Eyewitness
JUNGLE

Medicinal
calabar beans
*Physostigma
venenosum*

Eyewitness
JUNGLE

Written by
THERESA GREENAWAY

Photographed by
GEOFF DANN

White-lipped
tree frog
Litoria infrafrenata

*Clerodendrum
splendens*

Climbing fern
Leptochilus decurrens

Medicinal
Heckel
chewstick
Garcinia kola

Stone axe
(Guyana)

A Dorling Kindersley Book

Spear (Guyana)

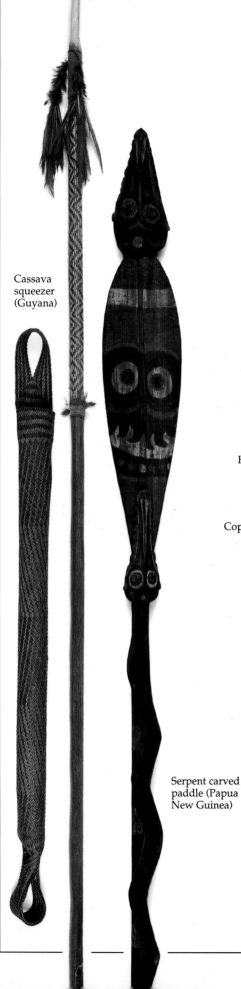

Cassava
squeezer
(Guyana)

Serpent carved
paddle (Papua
New Guinea)

Pacu
Colossoma oculus

DK

LONDON, NEW YORK, TORONTO, MELBOURNE, MUNICH, and DELHI

Project editor Miranda Smith
Art editors Andrew Nash & Sharon Spencer
Managing editor Simon Adams
Managing art editor Julia Harris
Production Catherine Semark
Picture research Kathy Lockley
Research Céline Carez

PAPERBACK EDITION
Managing editor Andrew Macintyre
Managing art editor Jane Thomas
Category publisher Linda Martin
Art director Simon Webb
Editor and reference compiler Sue Nicholson
Art editor Andrew Nash
Production Jenny Jacoby
Picture research Deborah Pownall
DTP designer Siu Yin Ho
2 4 6 8 10 9 7 5 3

This Eyewitness ® Guide has been conceived by
Dorling Kindersley Limited and Editions Gallimard

Hardback edition first published in Great Britain in 1994.
This edition published in Great Britain in 2003
by Dorling Kindersley Limited,
80 Strand, London WC2R 0RL

A CIP catalogue record for this book is
available from the British Library.

ISBN 0 7513 6488 6

Colour reproduction by
Colourscan, Singapore
Printed in China by Toppan Co.,
(Shenzen) Ltd.

Passionflower
Passiflora sp.

See our complete
catalogue at

www.dk.com

Contents

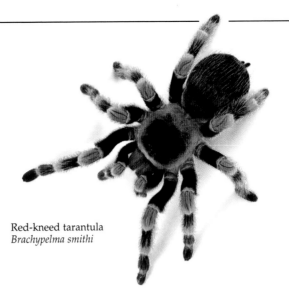

Red-kneed tarantula
Brachypelma smithi

What is a rainforest?

TROPICAL RAINFORESTS are perhaps the least understood and most valuable of the world's ecosystems. They are structurally complex, ages old, and have a climate that allows year-round growth. They contain a larger diversity of plants and animals than anywhere else on earth – for example, there are 50-200 different kinds of trees in one hectare of rainforest alone. These jungles have three layers – an evergreen canopy in the middle, a layer of smaller plants on the forest floor and, towering above the canopy, scattered taller trees known as emergents. The speed at which the vegetation grows and fills any gap or forest clearing impresses modern visitors as much as it did the early explorers. Rainforests all around the world are amazingly uniform in many respects. Similar niches on different continents have been filled by species that look alike but are quite unrelated.

COLOUR IN THE CANOPY
Splashes of colour in the canopy may indicate that a tree has burst into flower. It is just as likely that a flush of red, orange, pink, or white new leaves has unfurled.

NORTH AMERICA

RUSSIA

Tropic of Cancer

INDIA

AFRICA

Equator

SOUTH AMERICA

Tropic of Capricorn

AUSTRALIA

Palm tree

Undergrowth

☐ Rainforest area

WARM AND VERY WET
Tropical rainforests are found in permanently wet, warm areas near the Equator. There are at least 1,500 mm (60 in) of rain a year, with little or no dry season. The rain falls almost every day, in torrential downpours of outsize raindrops. The average temperature is around 25°C (77°F) and there is little seasonal variation.

THE FOREST FLOOR
Swamp forest soils are regularly enriched by silt-laden flood waters. Away from flooded areas, much of the lowland forest has surprisingly poor, infertile soils called oxisols. Nutrients are locked up in living plants and animals until released by organisms such as termites and fungi.

Tall emergent tree

Green-winged
macaw

At the top

Canopy

Black-and
white-colobus

Queen Alexandra's
birdwing

Liana

Forest canopy

Cuvier's toucan

White–lipped
tree frog

Young sapling

Forest floor

Red–kneed
tarantula

RAINFOREST IN THREE STOREYS
This model shows many of the features shared by all
lowland tropical rainforests. The trees have straight trunks, with
no branches for much of their height, and are supported by buttress
roots. Climbing plants, or lianas, climb up the trees, or they start life
lodged in the canopy and send roots down to the earth below. At ground
level, a luxuriant growth of plants springs up wherever the light reaches.

Types of rainforest

THERE ARE A NUMBER of different types of tropical forest. Lowland rainforest covers the greatest area, and is found in the warm, wet lowlands where there is little or no dry season. Seasonal, or monsoon forest also has a heavy rainfall, but it is not evenly distributed throughout the year. There is a dry season of three months or longer, during which the trees shed their leaves. Lianas and epiphytes do not grow here, as they cannot survive the dry conditions. Tropical mountainsides are thickly forested, but on the upland slopes, lowland rainforest becomes montane forest, which is divided into lower montane, upper montane, and elfin forest. Elfin forest is a miniature landscape of stunted, gnarled trees, shrouded in mist and covered with mosses and liverworts. Sometimes the division between rainforest types is clear, but often two rainforest types merge so there is no clear boundary.

MONTANE FOREST
In Malaysia, lowland rainforest gives way to lower montane forest at altitudes of about 1,000 m (3,280 ft). The climate is cooler, but still moist. There is dense tree cover, but the height of the canopy gets lower and lower. The trees have smaller leaves and tree ferns are abundant, as are magnolias, rhododendrons, myrtles, and laurels.

CLOUD FOREST
At higher altitudes, a permanent heavy mist envelops the forest. The climate of cloud forests, such as the Maquipucuna Reserve in Ecuador, is cool and very damp. Moisture in the mists condenses on the surface of the leaves and constantly drips from them. Mosses and liverworts cover everything with a spongy blanket. Because of the lower temperatures, the leaf litter decomposes very slowly. A thick layer builds up on the ground, eventually turning into peat.

Montane

Lowland

Mangrove

Height at which montane forest replaces lowland forest is variable

RAINFOREST LEVELS
Lowland rainforest can reach right down to the coast. Wherever there are the right conditions, mangrove forest extends along the coast and into river estuaries. With every 100 m (328 ft) increase in altitude, there is a drop in temperature of about 0.6°C (1.1°F).

LOWLAND RAINFOREST
Viewed from the river, the Rio de Los Amigos, the structure of this lowland rainforest in Peru is clearly visible. In the foreground, young climbers, ferns, and saplings flourish in the increased light levels beside the river. A cycad, a remnant of a truly ancient group of plants, also grows in this clearing. Tall palms make up a large proportion of the canopy. Towering over them are the umbrella-shaped crowns of the rainforest's huge emergent trees.

Scarlet ibis
Eudocimus ruber
(South America)

LIVING IN A SWAMP

Perhaps the most spectacular inhabitant of South American mangrove swamps is the scarlet ibis. It nests and roosts in large colonies. By day, it feeds on tidal mudflats or in the shallow waters of lagoons or beaches, probing for shellfish and worms with its long bill. As dusk approaches, a whole flock wheels and circles against the sky before flying into the mangroves to roost.

STILT ROOTS

The palm *Verschaffeltia splendida* is found naturally only in the rainforests that cover the steep hillsides of the Seychelles Islands. There, the wet, rocky ground has a thin layer of soil. Thick stilt roots grow out from the lower part of the trunk. They give the palm firmer anchorage on difficult terrain.

*Verschaffeltia
splendida*
(Africa)

MANGROVES

Deep layers of mud and silt accumulate along sheltered tropical coastlines and in river estuaries. A number of different kinds of trees, collectively known as mangroves, colonize these muddy shores and form swampy forests. The mud and the warm, shallow seawater that ebbs to and fro are very low in oxygen. So that their roots can breathe, mangroves have pneumatophores, roots that stick up above the mud and take in oxygen from the air through large pores or lenticels. The *Rhizophora* pneumatophores (above) grow in a tangle of arches; others are like knobbly knees or narrow spikes.

*New stilt root
growing out
from trunk*

*Splayed out stilt
roots improve
anchorage*

At the top

TALL EMERGENT TREES tower above the rest of the jungle canopy, a few reaching heights of 60-70 m (200-230 ft). These scattered trees have straight trunks, often buttressed at the base and with a cauliflower-shaped crown. It is hotter and drier at the top of the canopy, with greater changes in temperature and humidity. The trees are also much more windblown, and the fruit or seeds of some species are dispersed by the moving air. Many emergent trees are leafless for short periods of time, but seldom all shed their leaves at once. The epiphytes that live on the boughs of these trees include drought-resistant species of bromeliads, lichens, and cacti.

MONKEY BUSINESS
The striking black-and-white colobus monkey lives right at the top of the jungle, feeding on leaves.

PENANG FOREST
Tualang trees (*Koompassia excelsa*) often reach 70 m (230 ft) – but an 87 m (285 ft) tualang holds the record for a broadleaved rainforest tree. Malaysians believe that spirits live in these trees.

Sun conure
Aratinga solstitialis
(South America)

FLYING FORAGER
Conures live in noisy flocks high up in the tree tops. They fly restlessly from tree to tree, feeding on flowerbuds, fruits, seeds, and insects. They often eat unripe seeds.

Leaves have a waxy surface

GREEN SHADES
The tall canopy tree *Carapa guianensis* belongs to the mahogany family, and is found predominantly in swampy or seasonally flooded parts of the forest. Mature trees may produce 300 or more large, corky fruits that split into four segments, each containing 2-3 large seeds. Most of these are eaten by animals.

Carapa guianensis
(Central and South America)

EAGLE-EYED
One of the world's largest eagles, the harpy leaves its post in a tall emergent tree to swoop with speed and agility through the canopy. Its exceptionally strong legs and immense talons are used to snatch howler monkeys or sloths, wrenching them free from a tightly grasped branch. Harpy eagles use the same nest site every year. They build a bulky nest of sticks lined with leaves and fur in the boughs of an emergent kapok tree, 50 m (165 ft) or so above the ground.

Harpy eagle
Harpia harpyja
(Central and South America)

Rhipsalis baccifera
(South America)

*Small,
white fruit*

CACTUS AT THE TOP
Its fleshy, leafless stems mean that this epiphytic cactus can survive the long, hot dry spells between downpours. The small white fruits have a sticky pulp that helps them adhere to the bark.

*Young
developing leaf*

Abarema idiopoda
(Central America)

Bi-pinnate leaf

LEAF DIVISION
Rainforest trees have large leaves. These are either simple leaves with a waxy surface and a smooth outline, or leaves which are divided into separate leaflets. *Abarema* is bi-pinnate – its leaves are twice divided and have small leaflets. *Carapa and Abarema* are leafless for brief periods, normally when there is a dry spell, or the tree is flowering.

Forest canopy

LIFE IN THE CANOPY
This male tawny rajah (*Charaxes bernardus*) is one of many kinds of butterfly that may spend their entire life-cycle up in the forest canopy.

I N THE CANOPY of a rainforest, 25-45 m (80-150 ft) above the ground, it is always green and leafy. The crown of each tree is taller than it is broad, making a sun-speckled layer 6-7 m (20-23 ft) thick. This leafy roof shields the ground and absorbs most of the sunlight. It also lessens the impact of heavy rainfall and high winds. The teeming life of a jungle canopy is only glimpsed from below. Some creatures are so adapted to their tree-top existence that they seldom, if ever, descend to the forest floor. It is difficult even to match up fallen fruits or flowers with the surrounding tree trunks. Many species were totally unknown – or their numbers grossly underestimated – before walkways strung up in the canopy allowed biologists to find out what life was really like in the tree tops.

SAFE ASLEEP?
Canopy-dwelling creatures such as this silky anteater (*Cyclopes didactylus*) need to cling tightly to the branches. Sharp claws and a long, prehensile tail are adaptations shared by quite unrelated canopy animals.

REACHING THE HEIGHTS
Lianas are plants that need a lot of light, which they have to compete for against tall rainforest trees. By using these trees for support, the lianas do not invest energy and materials in a thick trunk of their own. Instead, their slender climbing stems reach the canopy, and the light, very quickly. Once up among the branches, they loop through the treetops, growing leaves, flowers, and fruit.

Liana
Clerodendrum splendens
(Africa)

White-lipped tree frog
Litoria infrafrenata
(Australasia)

STICKY-TOED TREE TRAVELLER
To avoid the hottest part of the day, thin-skinned tree frogs hide in damp, leafy crevices among canopy epiphytes. The smaller tree frogs may spend their entire lives in the canopy, even breeding in the reservoirs of water trapped by bromeliad leaves. Others, such as this white-lipped tree frog, laboriously make their way down to forest pools to mate and spawn. Long legs and sticky toe pads enable them to climb with consummate ease.

Cecropia glaziovii
(Central and South
America)

CANOPY FOLIAGE
The large leaves of lowland rainforest trees may
be simple in shape, or divided into leaflets or
lobed. The canopy remains leafy all year, but
within it, some trees shed their foliage
for short intervals – sometimes
as little as a few days.
Leaf-fall usually coincides
with the driest time
of the year, but it
is not always
synchronized,
even in trees
of the same
species.

Large lobed leaf

DRIP TIPS
This typical rainforest leaf has
a shiny, waxy surface, and it
is drawn out into a narrow
point, or drip-tip. Both these
features are designed to
encourage rainwater to run
off quickly. This prevents
the growth of minute
algae and liverworts.

FLEETING BEAUTY
Completely invisible from the ground,
epiphyte-laden boughs are like tree-top
gardens. Of all the different plants
perched on these branches,
orchids are among the
most fascinating. The
perfect white orchids
(right) last just
one day.

One-day orchid
Sobralia sp.
(Central America)

Ficus religiosa
(South-East Asia)

INSECT LIFE
Only some canopy insects have been
classified and named, like this click
beetle (*Chalculepidium sp.*). Even
then, little is known about them.

The forest floor

HEAVY WITH MOISTURE, the air near the shady forest floor is still and sultry. Only about two per cent of the light reaching the canopy penetrates the thick blanket of foliage. This dim light inhibits the growth of tree seedlings and other light-demanding plants. In the deepest jungle, the ground is a maze of roots littered with fallen leaves, twigs and branches. When a tree crashes down, the scene is very different – the extra light allows an upsurge of saplings, herbaceous plants, and lianas. Rates of growth are impressive; giant bamboos grow 23 cm (9 in) a day.

FOREST FUNGI
Bacteria, moulds, and fungi such as this *Marasmius* grow very quickly in the humid conditions of the forest floor. A mass of fungal threads called a mycelium takes nutrients from the litter of dead leaves, and spores are produced by the brightly coloured toadstools.

SHADE-LOVER
Each long-stalked leaf of *Alocasia thibautiana* has silvery veins on top, and is purple underneath. Clumps of these shade-loving aroids can grow in the gloomiest parts of South-East Asian jungles – on the forest floor, beside streams, and even in the entrances of limestone caves.

A SPLASH OF COLOUR
A luxuriant growth springs up wherever there is enough light. Heliconias, with their bright red flowerheads, are widespread in Central American jungles.

TRAPPING LIGHT
The leaves of *Fittonia* contain red pigments that trap light and make good use of the dim conditions. Amerindian tribes use the plant to treat a variety of ailments.

Diplazium proliferum
(South-East Asia)

Fittonia albivenis
(South America)

FLOURISHING
Ferns thrive best where it is warm and damp, and many tolerate low light levels, so they are abundant on the jungle floor. This fern produces bulbils on its fronds which will sprout and take root, either when they are knocked off, or when the frond dies.

BURROWING WORM
The black-and-white amphisbaenid (*Amphisbaena fuliginosa*) is neither a lizard or a snake. It is a wormlike reptile that lives in burrows in the damp soil and leaf litter of the forest floor. It feeds on worms and other invertebrates, detecting prey by touch.

Banded pitta
Pitta guajana
(Malaysia)

BROWSING BIRD
The pitta finds invertebrates on the forest floor, using its good eyesight and sense of smell. It breaks snail shells on rocks.

BUTTRESS ROOTS
These enormous roots are characteristic of lowland tropical rainforest. The curving shapes rise from lateral roots that run at or near the surface of the ground. Buttress roots may spread up the trunk to 9 m (30 ft), forming supporting wings of particularly hard wood.

In the water

THE RAINFOREST is awash with water. It drips from the leaves, collects in puddles, runs down mountainsides, and eventually drains into huge, meandering rivers. The Amazon is the largest river of all – together with its tributaries, which number 1,000 or more, it holds two-thirds of the world's fresh water. There is an incredible diversity of life supported by this vast water system. It contains around 5,000 species of freshwater fish, and there may be another 2,000 awaiting discovery. Where rainforest rivers flood, they spread nutrient-rich silts over the surrounding land, creating swamp forests. When they join the sea, more silt is deposited in estuaries and deltas, contributing towards mangrove swamps.

WELL CAMOUFLAGED
Lurking immobile in shallow water, the craggy carapace of the matamata (*Chelus fimbriatus*) looks like a rock. This Amazonian turtle has nostrils at the tip of its long, uptilted snout which is used like a snorkel as it lies in wait for prey.

Leaf

Epidermis

Air-filled spongy tissue

Petiole

WATER HYACINTH
To keep the water hyacinth afloat, and the right way up, the base or petiole of each leaf stalk is swollen into an air-filled float. Cutting this in half reveals that each float is made up of a mass of air-filled spongy tissue. The leaf and stem are encased in a smooth, tough skin, or epidermis.

RUNNING ON WATER
The Jesus Christ lizard runs fast using its tail as a counterbalance. It has flattened scales and a flap of skin on its hind toes to increase surface area, so it can run on water to chase prey or escape danger.

Long tail used as extra leg on land

Large back feet stop lizard sinking on water

Jesus Christ lizard
Basiliscus basiliscus
(Central America)

Pacu
Collossoma oculus
(South America)

FRUIT-EATING FISH
The varzea and the igapo are two areas of swamp forest flooded every year by the Amazon. Fruits falling from palms and other trees attract fish such as the pacu.

Water hyacinth
Eichhornia crassipes

DANGER IN THE WATER
Formidably armed with rows of sharp, triangular teeth, the fiercely predatory piranha is dangerous only in the dry season when water levels are low and the fish gather in shoals of 20 or more. By feeding collectively, the fish are able to tackle large animals, although their usual prey is other fish, molluscs, fruits, or seeds.

Piranha
Serrasalmus niger
(South America)

FLOATING PLANT
The water hyacinth (above) floats with its feathery roots dangling down into the water. The plants grow very quickly, forming large rafts on the surfaces of lakes and slow streams. Smaller clumps are dispersed by the wind, blown along like small, unsinkable sailing ships.

Green anaconda
Eunectes murinus gigas
(South America)

Smooth, shiny scales keep friction to a minimum when swimming

DANGER ON THE RIVER BANK

Few carnivores would tackle a large anaconda moving lazily along the river's edge. Anacondas keep close to swamps or streams, but they can also climb trees. Exceptional individuals have been recorded at 10 m (30 ft) or more, but most anacondas are smaller than this. They are excellent swimmers, preying on animals that come to the water to drink, and killing their prey by constriction and drowning. Younger anacondas are more likely to be preyed on, and use their swimming skills to escape. The females give birth to 23 cm (9 in) long live young in the water.

Underside yellow with black markings

Black blotches break up outline and are a good camouflage

Broad leaves to absorb sunlight

Large gill chamber fills with water so oxygen from the water can be used to breathe when on land

Mud-skipper
Periophthalmus barbarus

SWAMP PLANT

Air-spaces in the leaves keep the water lettuce rosette buoyant. Each leaf is covered in a layer of water-repellent hairs, and is waterproof. New rosettes sprout from stolons that grow out sideways.

Water lettuce
Pistia stratiotes

Finely branched roots

LAND CREATURES?

When the tide goes out, the mudskipper stays behind on the exposed mudflats of mangrove swamps. Using its fins for support and balance, it flips its body rapidly from side to side, skipping across the mud.

SHOVEL-NOSED CATFISH

Hiding beneath water plants by day, this fish (right) forages on the river bed at night. Three pairs of long sensory barbels help it to feel its way around. The catfish pokes its long, flattened snout into mud and debris to scavenge for food, as well as taking live prey such as worms and small fish.

Shovel-nosed catfish
Sorubium lima
(South America)

Epiphytes

UP IN THE RAINFOREST tree tops, a special group of plants clothe the branches so thickly that the bark is completely hidden. These plants are called epiphytes, or air plants. They anchor themselves to the stems, trunks, branches, or even leaves of other plants. They do not take either water or food from their hosts. Instead they use them simply as a means of reaching the light. After heavy rain, the combined weight of epiphytes and the water they have trapped can be enough to bring down whole branches. In the wettest forests, up to 25 per cent of flowering plants and ferns are epiphytes, and there are many more kinds of mosses, liverworts, and lichens. The highest number of epiphytic species are found in Central and South American forests.

PLATYCERIUM
The bracket fronds of this large epiphytic fern loosely clasp the tree trunk, so that a litter of plant debris collects behind it. This compost is moistened by rainwater trickling down the trunk and a rich humus develops into which the fern grows roots. Hanging clear of the trunk are the fertile, spore-bearing fronds.

Leaf

Tillandsia juncea
(Central America)

Stanhopea martiana
(Central America)

Pendant flowers

Pseudobulb

Dischidia lanceolata
(Asia) *has flowers that stick clumps of pollen onto the legs or body of insect pollinators*

Velamen

Living root tissue

Aerial root

ORCHIDS
Epiphytic orchids are abundant in rainforests. Many have pseudobulbs, or 'false bulbs'. These are swollen segments of stem in which water is stored. *Stanhopea* orchids have tightly packed clusters of ridged pseudobulbs, each one with a single leaf.

AERIAL ROOTS
All orchid roots are surrounded by a thick, spongy layer, the velamen. The velamen soaks up water and dissolved nutrients. Although some of this is gradually absorbed, most stops the roots from drying out. Even after the water has evaporated, the white walls of the empty velamen cells reflect light and heat, so protecting the living root tissues.

Anthurium salviniae
(Central America)

*This aroid has leaves
that channel water down to a
detritus-catching mat of roots*

*This plant absorbs water
from the air through
scales on the leaves*

WATER TANKS
Epiphytic bromeliads, or urn
plants, are found in New World
rainforests. Each plant has a
rosette of stiff leaves around a
short stalk. The tightly overlapping
leaf bases form a series of cups that
collect rainwater. Plant fragments
also become trapped, releasing
nutrients into the water as they
rot. Both water and dissolved
minerals are absorbed by the bromeliad
through specialized hairs on the leaf
surface. These high-rise pools support an
incredible number of aquatic insects and
invertebrates. Some frogs even breed in them.

Aechmea fasciata
(South America)

*An aroid with silver-
veined leaves that have
a velvety upper surface*

Anthurium crystallinum
(South America)

Branching out

Heavy rain soon drains
through the canopy,
and the sunshine,
although patchy,
is very hot. This
means that water and
dissolved nutrients can be
in short supply. Because of
this, epiphytes share many
of the characteristics of plants
that grow in arid conditions.
The leaves have a thick, waxy,
waterproof outer layer to reduce
evaporation and are arranged so that
rainwater is funnelled to the roots. The
decomposing organic remains caught in
water traps provide a source of fertilizer.

Oncidium excavatum
(South America)

Tillandsia usneoides
(Central America)

*Young seedlings
like this have
anchoring roots;
the mature air
plants are a tangle
of stems and very
narrow leaves*

Guzmania lingulata
(Central America) *is a
bromeliad that prefers shade*

*Aechmea
purpurea-rosea*
(Brazil)

Climbers

ONE OF THE MOST impressive features of a tropical forest is the abundance of climbing plants, or lianas. Some lianas grow to a huge size, with long stems that climb in search of light to the forest canopy, looping from branch to branch and linking the crowns of trees. Once up in the canopy, they develop branches that bear leaves and flowers. Lianas also send aerial roots down to ground where the roots bury themselves in the soil. These long roots become woody, and in turn act as supports for climbers that twine, or cling on with tendrils.

BLACK SPIDER MONKEY
Spider monkeys spend all their time in the trees, using their long limbs and tail to grip the branches.

Rhaphidophora decursiva

ROOT CLIMBERS
These climbers cling to the bark with roots that come out at right angles from the nodes all along the stem. They either press into the crevices of rough bark, or grow round a smooth surface. As the plant gets larger, aerial roots also sprout from the nodes. These are feeding roots that go straight down to the ground.

Node

TENDRIL CLIMBERS
Vines like *Teratostigma* send out straight tendrils that bend away from the light, sweeping slowly around until they come into contact with a stem or leaf. This causes the tendril to coil tightly. It does this very quickly, wrapping itself round a supporting stem in a few minutes.

Teratostigma (South-East Asia)

Rhaphidophora decursiva (South-East Asia)

Aerial root

Mesh

Fig

STRANGLERS
Strangler figs destroy host trees when they grow. They begin life as epiphytes, and become very tall trees with hollow trunks.

The fig sends aerial roots to the ground, where they spread through the soil

Roots grow branches that form a woody mesh round the trunk of the host

Fig kills the host tree by strangulation and by blocking out its light

Begonia serratipetala

GROWING TOGETHER
Strong climbing plants such as *Rhaphidophora decursiva* have juvenile leaves very different from the adult foliage. The young plants have short stems, with closely overlapping "shingle" leaves that press against the bark to prevent loss of water. Later, long-stalked adult leaves develop. In contrast, the climbing *Begonia serratipetala* is delicate and its leaves shrivel if exposed to dry air.

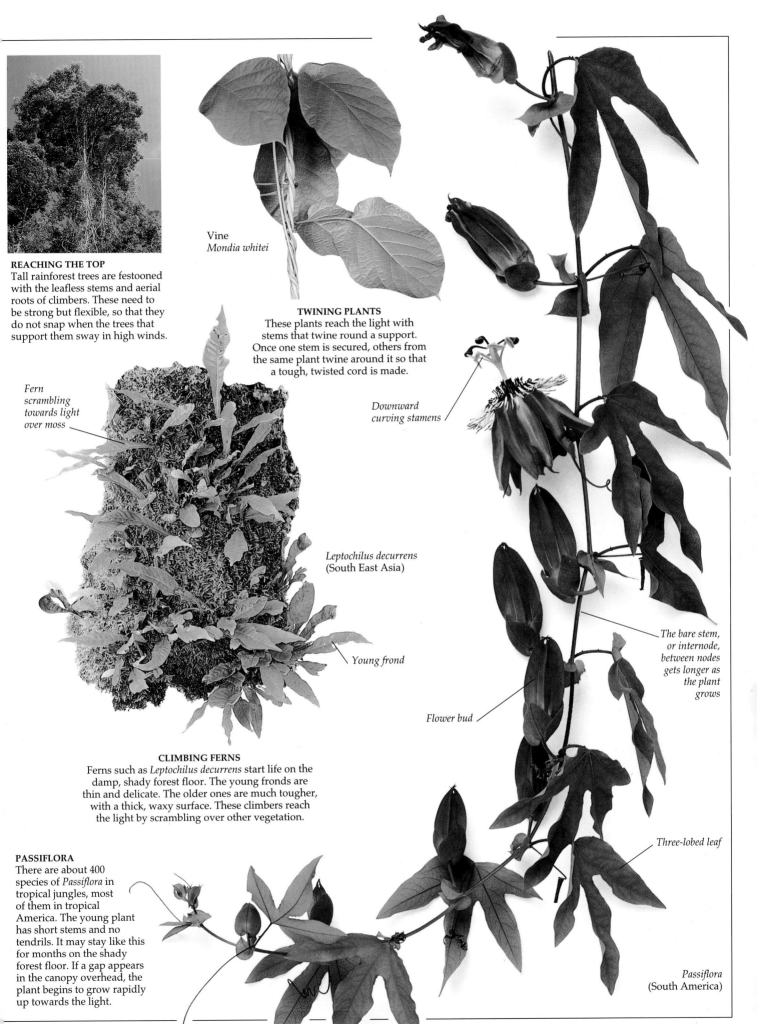

REACHING THE TOP
Tall rainforest trees are festooned with the leafless stems and aerial roots of climbers. These need to be strong but flexible, so that they do not snap when the trees that support them sway in high winds.

Vine
Mondia whitei

TWINING PLANTS
These plants reach the light with stems that twine round a support. Once one stem is secured, others from the same plant twine around it so that a tough, twisted cord is made.

Downward curving stamens

Fern scrambling towards light over moss

Leptochilus decurrens
(South East Asia)

Young frond

CLIMBING FERNS
Ferns such as *Leptochilus decurrens* start life on the damp, shady forest floor. The young fronds are thin and delicate. The older ones are much tougher, with a thick, waxy surface. These climbers reach the light by scrambling over other vegetation.

The bare stem, or internode, between nodes gets longer as the plant grows

Flower bud

PASSIFLORA
There are about 400 species of *Passiflora* in tropical jungles, most of them in tropical America. The young plant has short stems and no tendrils. It may stay like this for months on the shady forest floor. If a gap appears in the canopy overhead, the plant begins to grow rapidly up towards the light.

Three-lobed leaf

Passiflora
(South America)

Central American jungles

ONCE THE CENTRES of the great Maya and Aztec civilizations, the small countries bridging North and South America contain an incredible diversity of plant and animal life. A large number of plants native to the region are found nowhere else, and it is home to many important tropical crops, including pawpaws, allspice, vanilla, and avocado pears. Central America and the Caribbean islands are particularly rich in birdlife. The small country of Panama has more bird species than are found in the whole of North America, including migratory species that overwinter in the warm rainforests, returning to North America to breed.

ANCIENT CULTURE
The Maya civilization flourished in Belize and Guatemala until A.D. 800. They left many examples of intricately decorated pottery showing how they observed animals, such as this jaguar.

Epiphytic orchid
Stanhopea wardii

CARIBBEAN ISLANDS

Caribbean Sea

CENTRAL AMERICA

□ Former rainforest
▨ Actual rainforest

CENTRAL AMERICA
Before the 16th century, the Caribbean islands were almost completely covered with rainforest. Nearly all of this was cleared, island after island, to make way for sugar plantations. The rainforests of mainland Central America now cover only about 40 per cent of their original extent, with only Belize retaining as much as 60 per cent.

Sharp, poisonous spines to protect caterpillar from predators

Postman butterfly caterpillar
Heliconius melpomene

JUNGLE COLOUR
Different kinds of *Heliconia* grow in shady conditions beside streams or in overgrown clearings. The striking flowerheads are made up of brightly coloured bracts, each one enclosing a number of small flowers.

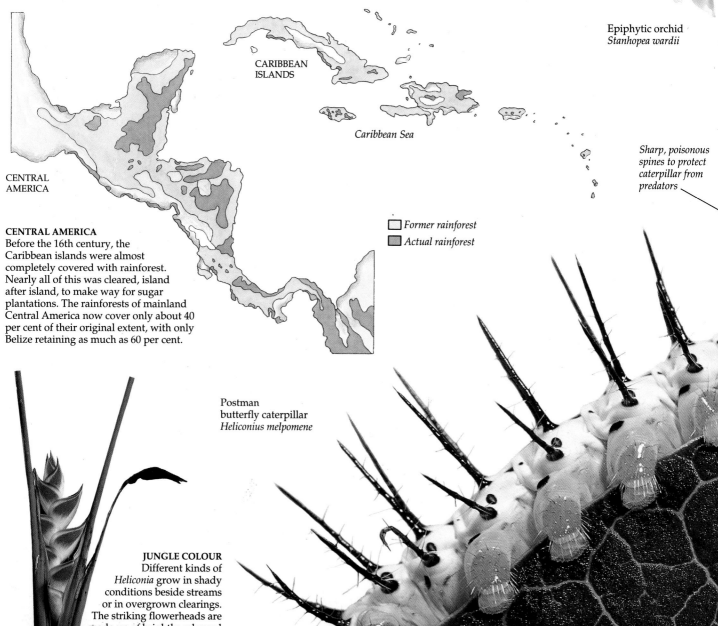

WELL NOURISHED
These butterflies are able to live for six to nine months because they feed on protein-rich pollen as well as nectar. They squirt enzymes onto the pollen which turns it into a "soup" that can be sucked up. Their longer life-span means that they can lay more eggs.

Winged central column

Postman butterfly
Heliconius melpomene

BRIEF BEAUTY
Hanging in fragrant sprays, the large waxy flowers of this lowland, epiphytic orchid are short-lived, withering after pollination. At the centre of its petals, each flower has a winged central column with fleshy lips, designed to attach the clumps of pollen firmly onto its euglossine bee pollinator.

Scarlet macaw
Ara macao

WINGS IN THE TREE TOPS
Raucous calls reveal the presence of these macaws in the tree tops. These brightly coloured and gregarious birds squabble over nesting sites, tree holes at least 30 m (100 ft) above the ground. Their diet consists mostly of seeds, many of which are protected by a hard shell. The macaw positions a seed in the upper part of its beak with its tongue, and cracks it with the lower mandible – just like a pair of pincers.

PROGRAMMED TO EAT
The postman butterfly caterpillar eats enormous numbers of leaves in the short time before it metamorphoses into a butterfly. Many different postman butterfly caterpillars feed on *Passiflora* vines. The female butterfly always selects young shoots or tendrils that do not already have eggs on them, as the first caterpillars to hatch will devour any younger ones.

JUNGLE GOLD
The golden beetle *Plusiotis resplendens* is about 3 cm (over 1 in) long and is only found in Costa Rica. The adult beetles eat leaves, but the larvae feed on soft, rotting plants.

Slipper orchid
Paphiopedilum callosum
(South-East Asia)

Sweet success

A FLOWER HAS TO BE POLLINATED before seeds can develop. Flowers are made up of petals around the male (stamens) and female (carpels) reproductive parts that produce its seeds. During pollination, pollen is transferred from the stamens to the stigma at the tip of a carpel. Pollination almost always happens between plants of the same species, and stamens and carpels are often arranged so that self-pollination is not possible. Most jungle plants are pollinated by insects, birds, or animals. In order to attract their pollinators, flowers offer sugary nectar or protein-rich pollen as food. They draw attention to themselves with brightly coloured petals or strong scents.

Line acting as nectar guide

Pouched petal

Short-tailed leaf-nose bat carrying baby
Anoura geoffroyi
(South America)

EXOTIC ORCHID
Tropical slipper orchids are often pollinated by a single species of bee or hoverfly. The insect is guided to the centre of the flower, where it is slippery, so it falls into a pouched petal. The only way out is to climb up hairs at the back of the pouch, a route that takes it past the stigma and pollen sacs. Pollen sticks to the insect and is carried to the female stigma of the next flower.

BAT POLLINATION
Bat-pollinated flowers such as *Pachira aquatica* open at dusk, just as the bats wake up. The bats are attracted to the flowers by a pungent or sour smell, and the flowers are arranged so that bats can reach them easily. As a bat drinks the nectar, its furry head is dusted with pollen from the long stamens.

Long stamens

NECTAR-SIPPER
Bats that feed exclusively on nectar have long tongues with a brushlike tip which quickly mops up pollen as well as droplets of nectar. These bats can hover while feeding.

Shaving brush tree
Pachira aquatica
(South America)

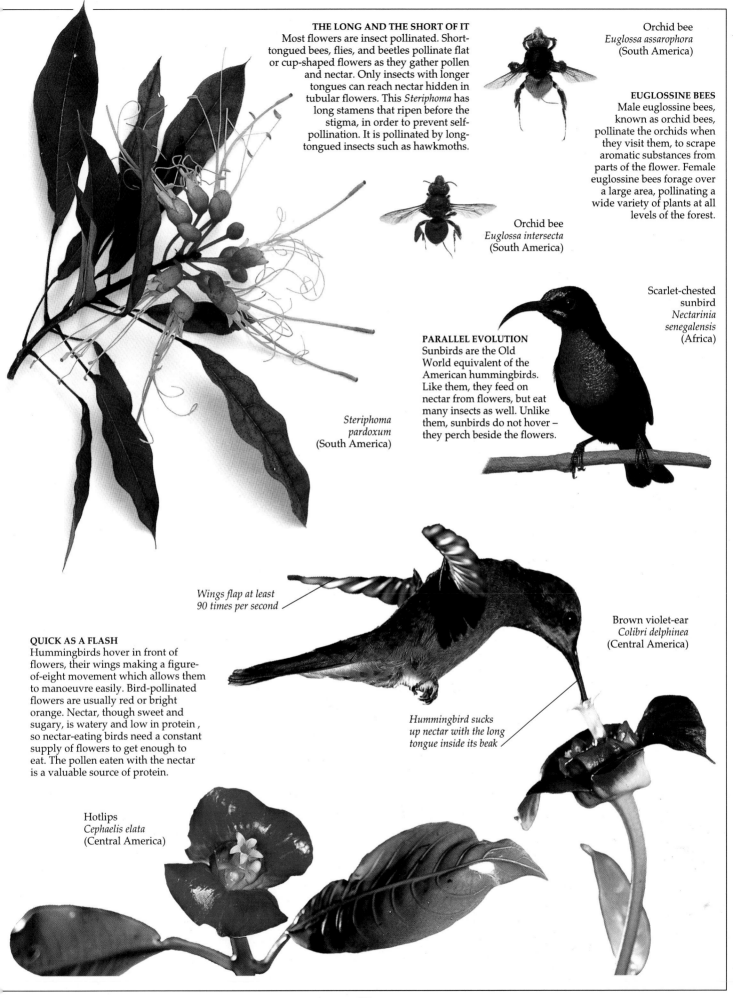

THE LONG AND THE SHORT OF IT
Most flowers are insect pollinated. Short-tongued bees, flies, and beetles pollinate flat or cup-shaped flowers as they gather pollen and nectar. Only insects with longer tongues can reach nectar hidden in tubular flowers. This *Steriphoma* has long stamens that ripen before the stigma, in order to prevent self-pollination. It is pollinated by long-tongued insects such as hawkmoths.

Orchid bee
Euglossa assarophora
(South America)

EUGLOSSINE BEES
Male euglossine bees, known as orchid bees, pollinate the orchids when they visit them, to scrape aromatic substances from parts of the flower. Female euglossine bees forage over a large area, pollinating a wide variety of plants at all levels of the forest.

Orchid bee
Euglossa intersecta
(South America)

Scarlet-chested sunbird
Nectarinia senegalensis
(Africa)

PARALLEL EVOLUTION
Sunbirds are the Old World equivalent of the American hummingbirds. Like them, they feed on nectar from flowers, but eat many insects as well. Unlike them, sunbirds do not hover – they perch beside the flowers.

Steriphoma pardoxum
(South America)

Wings flap at least 90 times per second

Brown violet-ear
Colibri delphinea
(Central America)

QUICK AS A FLASH
Hummingbirds hover in front of flowers, their wings making a figure-of-eight movement which allows them to manoeuvre easily. Bird-pollinated flowers are usually red or bright orange. Nectar, though sweet and sugary, is watery and low in protein , so nectar-eating birds need a constant supply of flowers to get enough to eat. The pollen eaten with the nectar is a valuable source of protein.

Hummingbird sucks up nectar with the long tongue inside its beak

Hotlips
Cephaelis elata
(Central America)

Seed dispersal

HEALTHY APPETITE
The Asian great hornbill (*Buceros bicornis*) is an avid fruit-eater. Seeds germinate from its droppings.

PLANTS NEED to spread their seeds so that they have room to grow. Because they cannot move around, they rely on wind, animals, water, or explosive pods to scatter their seeds. The fruit wall is part of a plant's dispersal mechanism. Some fruits are winged or cottony to help the seeds become airborne. Some are air-filled and float on water. More familiar are the juicy, brightly coloured fruits that spread their seeds by enticing animals, including people, to eat their succulent flesh. These seeds are spread when animals spit them out, let them fall, or pass them out in droppings deposited some distance away.

Hard seed case

ATTRACTIVE MORSEL
This *Elaeocarpus angustifolia* seed was enclosed in a purple fruit with oily flesh. The fruit is swallowed whole by birds, such as hornbills.

RATTAN PALMS
Rattan palms produce clusters of fruits. These usually contain a single seed enveloped in a fleshy layer that is eaten by birds and animals. As hard shelled seeds pass through the digestive tract of an animal, their outer wall is eaten away by digestive juices. This means that water absorption and germination are easier.

Fruit is in clusters at base of frond

Rattan seeds
Calamus paspalanthus
(South-East Asia)

BURIED AND FORGOTTEN
Inside the fibrous case of *Loxococcus rupicola* is a hard nutty seed that is dispersed by rodents. These gnawing animals bury seeds for future feasts. Forgotten caches germinate and grow.

Red lemur palm fruit
Lemurophoenix halleuxii
(Madagascar)

A CASE THAT IS HARD TO CRACK?
Larger animals and fruit-eating bats often carry fruit to a safe place before eating it. Some seeds are then spat out or discarded, especially if they are too hard to crack.

Pigafetta filaris
(Australasia)

FRUIT-EATER
This lemur lives in tall trees beside rivers in southern Madagascar. Fruit is the most important part of its diet, although it also eats insects and leaves.

Ring-tailed lemur
Lemur catta
(Madagascar)

Hard, nutty seed

SCALY FRUIT
Pigafetta, sago, and rattan palms are closely related species with fruits enclosed in shiny, overlapping scales. Beneath a sago palm's scales is a corky layer which enables the fruit to float, thus dispersing its single seed. A sago palm dies after it has fruited.

Sago palm
Metroxylon sagu
(Australasia)

Epauletted fruit
bat eating wild fig
Epomophorus wahlbergi
(Africa)

Kapok
seed

Kàpok pod
Ceiba pentandra

FRUITFUL FIGS
Figs are found in all tropical
rainforests. They are a significant
part of the diet of many animals, including birds,
bats, and monkeys. To stop the small fig seeds being
destroyed by digestive juices, the fig flesh contains a
laxative that ensures the seeds pass through quickly.

BLOWING IN THE WIND
Towering above the forest
canopy, the kapok tree
employs the wind to
disperse its seeds. Each
fruit pod is up to 18 cm
(7 in) long. As it ripens,
the pod wall dries and
eventually splits,
releasing a mass of
shiny floss in which
the seeds are
embedded. As this
is blown far and
wide by the winds,
the seeds fall out.

*Pod burst open
to disperse seeds*

Nypa palm seed
Nypa fruticans
(South-East Asia)

*Fibrous
wall*

SEEDS AFLOAT
Seeds that are
spread by water
need a waterproof
layer to prevent them
becoming waterlogged.
They also need an air-
filled fruit wall to keep them
afloat. Nypa palms grow in
the brackish mud of mangrove
swamps. Their fruits have a thick
fibrous wall that enables them to float
for several months, during which time
the seed inside may start to germinate.

Dusk to dawn

NIGHT COMES SWIFTLY in the tropics. At about 6 pm, darkness falls – there are no lingering hours of twilight. As the sun sinks towards the horizon, daytime creatures return to their roosts or nests, and a new group of animals awakens. By dividing into day and night shifts, different species of animals that would otherwise compete for food and space are separated. The cooler night air brings out insects and amphibians with thin, moist skins, while small mammals and rodents hunt on the forest floor. Nocturnal animals are specially adapted, and many have huge eyes, or acutely sensitive ears and noses. Yet the jungle is never completely dark. The moon shines on clear nights. Fireflies flash through the trees, and on the forest floor, phosphorescent fungi glow eerily, until they are devoured by beetles.

NIGHT FEEDER
By day, Franquet's epauletted bats roost in small groups, hanging from thin branches usually 4-6 m (13-20 ft) above the ground. As night falls, they fly off to feed on fruit, large numbers often gathering in a heavily laden tree. Fruit bats have large eyes with good vision, but they locate ripe fruit with their keen sense of smell.

Franquet's epauletted bat
Epomops franqueti
(Africa)

Wings folded when roosting

FLYING HOME TO ROOST
Just before darkness falls, parties of toucans fly off to roost in selected trees. They look ungainly in flight, but although large, their colourful bills are very light in weight, and they fly strongly across clearings and over the tree tops. As dawn breaks, the flock once more takes to the air, to search for ripe fruit.

Large curved beak for picking and eating fruit

Cuvier's toucan
Rhamphastos cuvieri
(South America)

NIGHTLIGHTS
Fireflies are actually different species of beetles. Males of "roving" fireflies, such as *Pyrophorus* from tropical America, fly among the trees flashing in special sequences that are only answered by females of the right species.

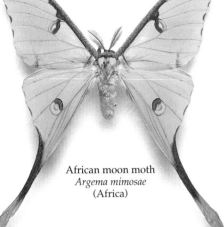

NECTAR-SIPPERS
Night-flying moths feed on the nectar of sweetly-scented, pale-coloured flowers, many of which are open only for a single night. This African moon moth is one of the largest species, with a wingspan of 12 cm (4 in). The feathery antennae of the male are so sensitive that they can pick up the slightest trace of the pheromone – sex hormone – wafting from a female moth.

African moon moth
Argema mimosae
(Africa)

BIG EYES
The vertical pupils of the red-eyed tree frog *Agalychnis callidryas* open up at night to help them see in the very low light levels. By day, the pupils become slits. The frogs live and feed up in the canopy, only coming down to streams for the female to absorb water before she lays her eggs.

DAWN CHORUS
Just before dawn breaks, howler monkeys set up a noisy chorus. The deafening howls can be heard over 1 km away, and are produced in a large larynx by air passing over the hyoid bone. Mature males, such as this one, make the loudest howl, amplified by the position they hold themselves in while calling. This loud early morning symphony is a warning to other groups of howlers not to come too close, and safeguards their food supply.

Large eyes for night vision

Red howler monkey
Alouatta seniculus
(South America)

NIGHT MONKEY
The douroucouli, or night monkey, is the only nocturnal monkey in the world. As night falls, douroucoulis emerge from tree holes to feed on fruit, leaves, insects, and other small animals. Their large, forwardly pointing eyes are typical of nocturnal primates, and help them to see in the near-darkness as they leap and climb from branch to branch.

Douroucouli
Aotus trivirgatus
(South America)

DIGGING DOWN
The scaly Indian pangolin *Manis crassicaudata* digs a burrow in which it spends the day, emerging at night to forage on the forest floor. Though its sight is weak, it has an acute sense of smell which it uses to locate ant and termite mounds. Breaking in with the long powerful claws on its forelimbs, the pangolin flicks its very long sticky tongue into chambers full of insects, eggs, and pupae. It is toothless, and the swallowed insects are ground up in the lower part of its stomach.

South American jungles

THE AMAZON BASIN covers a vast area, 6 million sq km (nearly 2.5 million sq miles), and is covered by the world's largest expanse of tropical rainforest. This jungle supports more species of plants and animals than anywhere else – about one fifth of the world's bird and flowering plant species, and about one tenth of all mammal species. No definite figure can be put on the number of different insects, because many have yet to be identified – or even discovered – by scientists. Amerindian tribes have lived in these forests for about 12,000 years, during which time they have built up a detailed and valuable knowledge of the jungle plants, many of which they use in their everyday lives.

Mouth of Amazon River

SOUTH AMERICA

☐ *Former rainforest*
☐ *Actual rainforest*

SOUTH AMERICA
The forests of the north-west were separated from the Amazonian forests two million years ago by the formation of the Andes Mountains. A few small patches are all that remains of the once continuous strip of forest along the Atlantic coast of Brazil.

BODY PAINTING
These Yanomamo girls belong to one of 143 tribal groups remaining in Amazonia. Body painting is popular, using a plant known as urucu or achiote in South America and annatto in Europe. The seeds are wiped directly onto the skin or boiled to make a paste. Each tribe has its favourite patterns.

Annatto
Bixa orellana

A WAXY SURFACE
Growing naturally beside rivers and round the edges of swampy areas, the Brazilian wax palm *Copernicia prunifera* is also cultivated in Brazil for the carnauba wax that covers the surface of its leaves. Carnauba is a top quality wax with a high melting-point of 70°C (161°F). It is used chiefly in the cosmetic and polishes industries. The wax flakes off leaves that have been picked and dried in the sun. That taken from the young leaves is known as "prime yellow", and about 1,300 leaves are needed to obtain 1 kg (2.2 lbs) of wax.

ONE OF MANY
The malachite butterfly is just one of more than 2,000 species of butterflies in the Amazonian jungles. They fly during the day, pausing to feed on over-ripe fruit fermenting on the forest floor.

Malachite butterfly
Metamorpha stelenes

GOLD IN THE FOREST
This beautiful golden monkey is found only in Atlantic coastal rainforests. Golden lion tamarins live in mature forest, where they forage for invertebrates, small animals, and fruit 3-10 m (10-30 ft) up in the liana-covered trees. They came near to extinction in the 1960s, because their habitat was being destroyed and hundreds were being exported as pets every year. Since then, captive breeding programmes established in Europe and the United States have resulted in the release of golden lion tamarins back into the wild.

Long tail for balancing

Golden lion tamarin
Leontopithecus rosalia

Buriti palm
Mauritia flexuosa

THE TREE OF LIFE
Nothing of this tall palm goes to waste. The Amerindians use it as a source of food, fibres, wood, cork, and thatching. Wine made from the vitamin C rich fruits is given to the elderly and sick.

NOT SO LAZY
Despite its name, the three-toed sloth *Bradypus tridactylus* is not a lazy animal. It is perfectly adapted to its life up in the canopy. There is little protein in its diet of indigestible foliage, and by hanging upside down, it conserves energy. Its strong claws lock tightly onto branches so it does not fall off even when asleep – or dead!

Amazon lily
Eucharis amazonica

MYSTERIOUS POWERS
The Amazon lily grows on the lower slopes of the Andes. The Kofan tribes of western Colombia and northern Ecuador boil the whole plant, including its bulb, to make a tea. This is drunk by men before they hunt monkeys, in the belief that it will make them more accurate with the blowpipe.

Beside the water

THE RIVERBANK IS THE DOMAIN of animals that live both on land and in water. The vegetation here is particularly dense, as the open expanse of water allows extra light to reach the ground. This mosaic of water, overhanging branches, and tangle of waterside ferns, sedges, and saplings provides an ideal environment for animals that live and breed on land but enter the water to hunt and feed. However, heavy rains sometimes cause a river to burst its banks, and this puts those animals nesting close to the water's edge at risk.

JAWS OF THE RIVERBANK
The saltwater crocodile *Crocodilus porosus* is the world's largest crocodile. It can reach 6 m (20 ft) in length and weigh as much as 3 tonnes.

UMBRELLA GRASS
The sedge *Cyperus alternifolia* has leaves that radiate from the top of its tall stems like the spokes of an umbrella. Underwater, the roots grow into an impenetrable tangle that helps to stabilize the edges of the swamps in which it grows.

WARY WATER LIZARD
Water dragons are agamid lizards that live beside water in the forests of South-East Asia and Australia. Although they are mainly tree-dwellers, they can run quickly over the ground on their two hind legs, usually aiming for the next tree. When not searching for invertebrates, eggs, and nestlings to eat, they spend most of their time resting along a branch overhanging the water. They are extremely wary and, at the slightest disturbance, will drop off into the water, which may be as much as 9 m (30 ft) below.

Crested water dragon
Physignathus sp.
(Asia)

WATERSIDE PLANT
The waterside plant *Thalia geniculata* is abundant in marshes and seasonally flooded ground near rivers. It has large, waxy leaves and spreads by means of tuberous roots.

An alert crested water dragon stands on all four feet, watching for danger

GIANT OTTER
Each family group of giant otters has its own territory. Ungainly on land, these creatures are excellent swimmers, using their large, webbed feet as paddles and their muscular tail as a rudder. They catch fish and carry it to the surface to eat.

FROGS IN DANGER
Originally inhabitants of Madagascan rainforests, these endangered tomato frogs, *Dyscophus autongili*, are now adapting to other habitats, as the forests dwindle in size.

Eyes on long stalks to spot danger while rest of the body is camouflaged

Fiddler crab
Uca vocans

Bat has a wingspan of 60 cm (24 in)

SWAMP DWELLER
The fiddler crab makes its burrow in the thick mud of mangrove swamps, emerging when the tide goes out. Only the males have a single, much enlarged front pincer. Useless for gathering food, it is used to signal alluringly to female crabs, and also to wrestle with rival males.

FISHING FOR FOOD
The fishing or bulldog bat *Noctilio leporinus* skims low over still water, using echolocation to detect ripples. It uses its sharply hooked claws to gaff fish out of the water. Its prey is either eaten on the wing or carried to a nearby roost.

Long tail for balance and to use as a rudder in water

Dry, scaly skin that is regularly shed, or sloughed off, to reveal a new layer

Powerful sharp-clawed feet for climbing

Hidden dangers

CURARE
The rough bark or roots of some *Strychnos* vines are ingredients of curare, used as an arrow poison by some tribesmen. In the past, each tribe had its own closely guarded secret recipe for making the poison.

Solid lump of prepared curare

LURKING IN THE DEPTHS of the jungle are animals and plants equipped with a lethal battery of foul-tasting poisons. They either manufacture the poisons themselves, or use those that were in their food, advertizing their hidden armoury with their bright colours. Venomous creatures such as snakes and spiders need powerful toxins to subdue prey that might inflict injury during a struggle. Plants contain poisons to prevent herbivores from eating all their foliage. The only indications that their green leaves are unpleasant are the smell and taste. They can afford to lose a few leaves, and animals soon learn to avoid them.

TAKING AIM
This Penan hunter in Borneo uses darts tipped with poisons. Different tribes use a variety of plant poisons to kill their catch quickly.

POTTED POISON
After the ingredients for curare are pounded together, the mixture is boiled or mixed with cold water. The thick liquid is strained off and kept in hollow gourds.

Arrow tipped with coating of curare

Living with poisons

The poisonous nature of animals and plants are understood by the peoples who live in the jungle. Many highly toxic plants are in everyday use, both for hunting and, in far smaller doses, as medicines. Concoctions are used to tip arrows so that animals fall from the canopy close to the hunter. Poisonous leaves or sap are used to contaminate stretches of water so that many fish die at the same time.

Arrows used to hunt monkeys and other mammals

SAFETY TIPS
South American hunters tie their arrows together with cord and keep them securely in a bamboo quiver for safety. They have to be careful that they do not accidentally prick themselves with a poisoned tip.

Bamboo quiver

IMMUNE TO DANGER

A female postman butterfly lays her eggs on the youngest *Passiflora* leaves, because these contain the least poison. The larvae absorb the poisons into their bodies.

Small postman butterfly
Heliconius erato
(South America)

Blue poison dart frog
Dendrobates azureus
(South America)

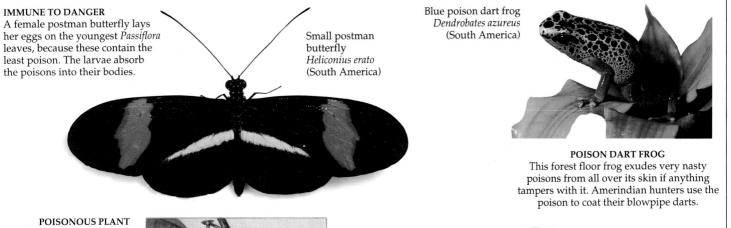

POISON DART FROG

This forest floor frog exudes very nasty poisons from all over its skin if anything tampers with it. Amerindian hunters use the poison to coat their blowpipe darts.

POISONOUS PLANT

If a plant loses most or all of its leaves, its ability to take in carbon dioxide and manufacture sugars is greatly reduced. The foliage of this large *Passiflora* climber contains a complex cocktail of chemicals including bitter-tasting alkaloids and compounds that contain cyanide. Mammals will not eat it, and only a few leaf-eating insects such as postman butterflies and some species of beetles have evolved ways of overcoming its toxicity.

Thai monocled cobra
Naja kaouthia
(South-East Asia)

Eyes set at side of head

Characteristic hood

Giant tiger centipede
Scolopendra gigantea
(Africa)

FATAL FEET

Dramatic orange and black stripes warn of this centipede's toxicity. It injects its prey with poisonous venom, using the first pair of its many legs, which have sharply tipped claws.

SUDDEN DEATH

This cobra is greatly feared. It inhabits buildings and scrubland as well as dense jungle, hunting at dusk and in the early morning. It takes prey, such as other reptiles and small mammals, by striking and gripping with front fangs that inject a highly toxic venom. This venom is also fatal to people, acting quickly on the nerves of the human respiratory system and the heart. When threatened, cobras rear up, hiss, and expand their "hood" by raising the elongated ribs of the neck region.

Nature's architects

THE RAINFOREST PROVIDES tree holes, tangles of lianas, and plenty of other hideaways. In spite of this, numerous creatures build custom-made homes from forest materials. Social insects such as bees, wasps, ants, and termites construct elaborate nests where a teeming mass of insects live and tend their larvae. These large colonies need well-protected structures to keep predators out. Some structures last for years. Birds are master weavers, but their nests are only used to rear young. Even less permanent are the beds made by gorillas. Every night, they prepare a mattress of leaves on the ground or among low branches.

THE CUTTING EDGE
Leaf-cutter ants live in underground nests in colonies of up to five million. "Media" workers only 10 mm long travel right up into the canopy, where they snip out neat pieces of leaf with their jaws. A continuous trail of ants carries these like flags back to the nest. There, 2 mm long "minima" workers chew the leaves to a paste, mixing it with faeces. This is used to grow the fungus on which the ants feed.

Ant domatia
Myrmecodia tuberosa

Scar left by fallen leaf

Stem is not lived in by ants

Thick, fibrous stem

CLOSE PARTNERSHIP
The relationship between *Iridomyrmex* ants and the epiphyte *Myrmecodia tuberosa* is just one of many fascinating jungle partnerships. The ants enter air spaces inside the plant through tiny holes in the plant wall. They establish their colony, rearing young and setting up fungus gardens. Fragments of dead plants and animals are brought in to nourish the fungus. The decaying matter then provides valuable internal compost for the host plant.

Airholes where ants enter

BAT CAMP
A few species of New World spear-nosed bats make their own daytime shelters from large leaves such as palm fronds and *Heliconia* foliage. They either bite a neat line across the veins of fan-shaped leaves, or along the midrib of long leaves, so that part of the leaf blade flops down. During the day, the bats roost in their green tents. Males are usually solitary, but females, such as these Honduran white bats (*Ectophylla alba*), cluster in small groups, especially while rearing their young.

Swollen base of plant

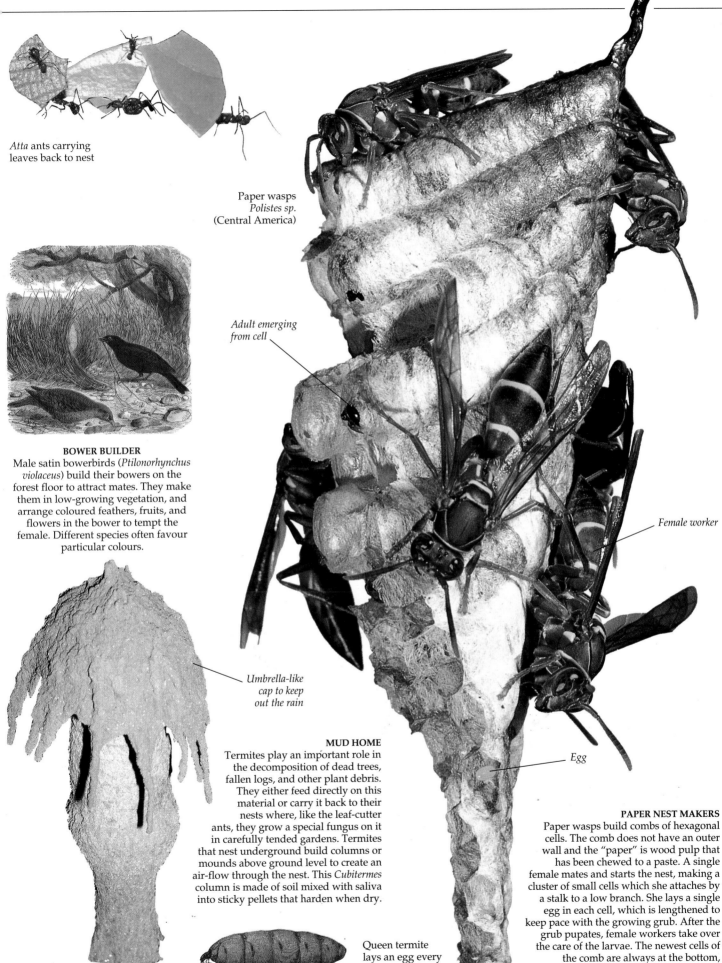

Atta ants carrying leaves back to nest

Paper wasps
Polistes sp.
(Central America)

*Adult emerging
from cell*

BOWER BUILDER
Male satin bowerbirds (*Ptilonorhynchus violaceus*) build their bowers on the forest floor to attract mates. They make them in low-growing vegetation, and arrange coloured feathers, fruits, and flowers in the bower to tempt the female. Different species often favour particular colours.

Female worker

*Umbrella-like
cap to keep
out the rain*

MUD HOME
Termites play an important role in the decomposition of dead trees, fallen logs, and other plant debris. They either feed directly on this material or carry it back to their nests where, like the leaf-cutter ants, they grow a special fungus on it in carefully tended gardens. Termites that nest underground build columns or mounds above ground level to create an air-flow through the nest. This *Cubitermes* column is made of soil mixed with saliva into sticky pellets that harden when dry.

Egg

Queen termite lays an egg every three seconds

PAPER NEST MAKERS
Paper wasps build combs of hexagonal cells. The comb does not have an outer wall and the "paper" is wood pulp that has been chewed to a paste. A single female mates and starts the nest, making a cluster of small cells which she attaches by a stalk to a low branch. She lays a single egg in each cell, which is lengthened to keep pace with the growing grub. After the grub pupates, female workers take over the care of the larvae. The newest cells of the comb are always at the bottom, although older cells are often re-used.

37

House and home

DEADLY WEAPONS
Tribes make their hunting
weapons from rainforest
materials. This spear
from Guyana is made
from feathers, wood,
bone, and basketry.
The palmwood bow is
strung with rattan,
and the three-tipped
fish arrow is made
of wood, bamboo,
reed, and cane.

WHEN PEOPLE NEED shelter, there
is no shortage of building materials
in the jungle. Slender tree trunks are
felled for use as walls, palm fronds are
cut for thatching, and tough cording
is prepared from lianas. Some tribes
build separate family homes grouped
together in a forest clearing. Others
favour one enormous structure that
houses the whole community, and
inside which each family has its own
hearth. Styles vary, but the houses
share some features, such as an
overhanging thatched roof to keep out
the rain. Inside, each dwelling contains
everyday utensils and weapons, made
skilfully from natural materials such
as bamboo and cane.

POTTER'S ART
The neolithic Kintampo culture brought
pottery to the African rainforests.
Containers such as this part-glazed pot
from lower Zaire are still made today.

*String made
of rattan*

*Bow made
of palm*

Model of a rainforest
house without walls
(South America)

WELL SHIELDED
Warring tribesmen held
shields to parry blows from
spears or arrows. Today,
many use them more often
for ceremonial purposes. This
colourful shield from Borneo
is decorated on the front with
human hair. The reverse
depicts tigers and dragons,
symbols of strength and
invincibility.

*Sturdy tree
trunks form
basic structure*

Human hairs

Dyak shield
(Borneo)

Palmwood bow
and fish arrow
(Papua New Guinea)

HIGH AND DRY
This hill tribe house in northern Thailand has central living quarters. It is well screened from the rain by thatching that sweeps down on all sides. The house is set on poles above the ground to keep the floor dry. Outside, there is plenty of shelter beneath the roof for outdoor tasks.

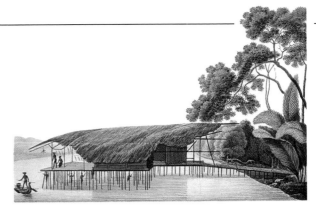

NATIVE HOUSE AT DORERI
Travelling by water is the easiest way to get round much of New Guinea because of the dense jungle vegetation. Many settlements are therefore built on the riverside or by the coast. This large house has been built on stilts over the water probably in order to escape destructive insects such as termites.

LIVING IN THE RAINFOREST
This model gives some idea of the the furniture and utensils found in a native rainforest house in South America. The occupants sleep in hammocks, knotted from cords. They weave lightweight vessels from cane or palm leaves, but heavy duty containers are made with strips of wood. Canoe paddles and weapons are also shaped from wood, and all of these items are stored by hanging them on the walls of the house. Clay pots are not made by all tribes, but are often acquired by trading.

Hammock

*Fishing
basket*

CHIEF'S YAM HOUSE
Yams are an important staple food. On the Trobriand Islands off the coast of New Guinea, yams are also a central part of complicated rituals that maintain goodwill and kinship between clans related by marriage. After the yam harvest, the chief's yam house is filled first. This brightly decorated house is thatched and has well-ventilated walls. This allows air to circulate, so that the yams do not go mouldy.

African jungles

STICKY FEET
The Madagascan day gecko (*Phelsuma madagascariensis*) has velcro-like toe pads so it can cling to branches – even running along underneath.

ALTHOUGH THEY CONTAIN an impressive 17,000 species of flowering plants, African rainforests have fewer species than those of either America or Asia. There are also fewer different kinds of ferns. This is because the climate of Africa became much drier during the last ice age, which ended about 12,000 years ago. Many animals and insects, as well as plants, died out during this period, surviving only in three well-separated pockets of forest that remained moist. As the ice retreated from the lands further north, the climate became wetter, and the surviving rainforest species spread out from their isolated refuges.

☐ *Former rainforest*
☐ *Actual rainforest*

AFRICA

Madagascar

AFRICA
More than 80 per cent of Africa's rainforest is in the central region. Along the coast of West Africa, the remaining forests are in fragmented pockets, but some countries are setting up conservation zones.

OIL PALM
This 10-20 m (33-65 ft) palm (*Elaeis guineensis*) yields two valuable oils – palm oil from the red, fibrous fruit pulp, and palm kernel oil from the seeds.

FLOWERS IN THE CANOPY
Of all the epiphytic flowering plants and ferns that grow in African jungles, over 60% are different kinds of orchids and little is known about their life histories. *Polystachya galeata* comes from Sierra Leone, where new reserves will help to safeguard its future and that of other vulnerable species.

FAST GROWTH
These large-flowered shrubs grow quickly up to 2 m (7 ft) tall. They flourish along the edges of the forest, where there is the most light. Their flowers attract bee and butterfly pollinators.

Hibiscus
Hibiscus calyphyllus

GOOD APPETITES
African elephants prefer to browse the dense vegetation of clearings and forest margins. Over half of their diet is foliage from trees and large climbers, but they will travel far into the depths of the jungle to reach their favourite tree fruits.

Black-and-white colobus
Colobus guereza
(Africa)

Senegal parrot
*Poicephalus
senegalensis*
(Africa)

FLASH OF COLOUR
The green and gold Senegal parrots migrate across savannah grassland into the forest to take advantage of ripening crops of fruits and seeds. They nest in unlined tree holes.

FAMILY GROUP
The guereza is one of four kinds of black-and-white colobus monkey that live in family groups in the tree tops. It is found in central and eastern Africa. Because these monkeys eat a wide range of readily available leaves, they do not need a very large home range.

*Only males have
a silver back*

*Large,
powerful
hands*

HEAD OF THE TRIBE
This silverback lowland gorilla *(Gorilla gorilla gorilla)* is a mature male. He is the dominant head of a social group that also contains mature females and young gorillas. Silverbacks are gentle with their young, but as their sons reach maturity, they have to leave and form their own social group. Gorillas travel slowly through the forest, eating leaves, stems, and shoots, and resting.

Wing stalked
yam powder

Medicines

MOST OF THESE PLANTS are very
poisonous. Yet, at the right dosage,
they help to alleviate suffering or save
lives. A rainforest can be compared to
a giant pharmacy where tribespeople
can find remedies for all their ills.
Only some of these medicinal plants
have been screened scientifically. It is
important to do this before either the
plants become extinct, or the tribes,
with their accumulated knowledge,
disappear. Many plants are known to
contain beneficial compounds. Others
have a more spiritual importance.
Some tribespeople think if a plant
looks like a bodily organ, it will cure
that organ of all ailments.

SKIN MEDICINE
Chaulmoogra ointment is a Hindu
preparation rubbed onto the skin to
treat leprosy and skin infections.

*Seed oil
is used in
chaulmoogra
ointment*

Hydnocarpus fruit and seeds
Hydnocarpus kurzii
(South-East Asia)

Wing stalked yam
Dioscorea alata
(South-East Asia)

INDIAN YAM
Yams are a good
source of diosgenin,
a compound used in oral
contraceptives. It is also used
in treatments for rheumatoid
arthritis and rheumatic fever.

Red cinchona bark
Cinchona succirubra
(South America)

Dried tongue of
pirarucu fish
(South America)

*Quinine stored
in the bark*

Guarana bark
Paullinia cupana
(South America)

HARD MEDICINE
This hard fruit comes from the *Hydnocarpus*
tree, grown in Burma, Thailand, and
India for its medicinal properties.

Heckel chew stick
Garcinia kola
(Africa)

PRECIOUS PLANT
The red cinchona
tree is one of four
commercial kinds
of *Cinchona*. The
quinine extracted
from the bark and
roots is an important
part of the treatment
of malaria, although
synthetic drugs are
also available today.

STIMULATING DRINKS
Guarana plants contain caffeine and
are made into tonic drinks all over
Brazil. Tribes grate the seeds
(above) or bark into water with
the rough, dried tongue of the
pirarucu fish. Strong, bitter doses
are used to get rid of intestinal
worms. The seeds are used
commercially in carbonated drinks.

Rosy periwinkle
Catharanthus rosea
(Africa)

Carved handle of chew stick

Entire seed

Seed with seed coat removed

Moreton Bay chestnut
Castanospermum australe
(Australasia)

A ROSY FUTURE
This one small plant gave hope to cancer sufferers when compounds were isolated from its leaves in the 1950s. Two alkaloids taken from its leaves – vincristine and vinblastine – are now used particularly in the treatment of Hodgkin's disease and childhood leukemia.

CHEW IT AND SEE
For centuries, in parts of Africa, tribespeople have used chew sticks to keep their teeth clean. Woods such as *Garcinia* and the toothbrush tree (*Salvadora persica*) release juices when chewed. These appear to act against bacteria in the mouth, cleaning teeth and preventing infection.

Seed pod of ouabain
Strophanthus hispidus
(Africa)

TAKING HEART
Ouabain was once used by African tribes as an arrow poison. Today, strophanthidin and sarmentogenin are extracted from the seeds of this plant. Strophanthidin is used to treat heart conditions. Sarmentogenin is the chemical starting-point for the manufacture of treatments for rheumatoid arthritis.

Seeds are wind dispersed

Seeds

Inside of seed case

Calabar bean
Physostigma venenosum
(Africa)

Seed kernel

Outside of seed case

Seedpod

KILL OR CURE?
The exceedingly poisonous seeds of the calabar bean were also known as ordeal beans, because they were used by Africans to decide the guilt of a person. If the eater survived, he or she was innocent. Extracts from the seeds are now used to treat glaucoma (a form of blindness) and high blood pressure.

MEDICAL ADVANCES?
The Aboriginals used to soak the seeds of the Moreton Bay Chestnut for a long time to make them edible. They were washing out the poison castanospermine. Research in the 1980s showed that this alkaloid has significant effects on some viruses, including the HIV that can cause AIDS.

Forest apes

THE TROPICAL RAINFORESTS are home to all
of the world's apes, and most of its monkeys,
although there are no primates in New Guinea
and Australia. So many species are able to live
close together because they inhabit different levels
in the forest canopy, or eat different food. Even
so, some groups are highly territorial: one of the
lasting impressions of the jungle is the sound
of monkeys and apes vociferously defending
their feeding area.

Very long arms

Jungle swinger

Gibbons like this siamang swing hand-
to-hand through the trees of the forest
canopy in a process called brachiation.
This is an effective way of moving very
quickly from tree to tree and is their
usual means of locomotion. They do fall
sometimes with fatal results, but it is the
most efficient way of finding the trees
that have ripe fruit to eat. Although
gibbons use brachiation most,
chimpanzees and some monkeys
also use this method.

Siamang
Hylobates syndactylus
(South East Asia)

*Opposable
big toe*

GOING FOR A WALK
A gorilla moves around the forest floor
on the flat of its feet and its knuckles
in quest of the vast quantities of
vegetation that it needs to eat
every day. Although normally
slow-moving, it is capable
of bursts of speed when
necessary, for example
when seeing off a rival.

Gorilla
*Gorilla
gorilla gorilla*
(Africa)

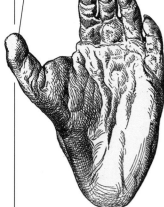

Gorillas have broad feet; the
big toes are opposable so
they can curl round to grip

Chimpanzees walk and
climb in lower canopy,
using both hands and feet

Gibbons spend all
their time up in trees
so have narrow feet

JUNGLE CHORUS
The siamang is the largest of the gibbons. Each
pair lives in the tree tops with their offspring. They
guard their territory and its vital food supply from
neighbouring siamangs with a morning and afternoon
duet of ear-splitting shrieks and barks. The loud calls,
which can be heard up to 1 km away, are given
extra resonance by their inflated throat sacs.

*Long, narrow hands
with thumb cleft
almost to the wrist*

*Forearm that
can rotate 180°*

*Shoulder joint
will rotate 360°*

*Powerful
shoulder
muscles*

*Leg outstretched to
maximize forward
movement*

Broad chest

*Legs curled up to increase
upward stroke of swing*

Legs shorter than arms

*Big toe long
and opposable*

CLEVER CHIMP
This primate is very good
with its hands. Most
chimpanzees use twigs
to get tasty morsels from
difficult places, but some
crack open nuts with
stones or branches. They
carry their 'hammers'
for long distances.

Chimpanzee
Pan troglodytes
(Africa)

Mandrill
*Mandrillus
sphinx*
(Africa)

Humboldt's
monkey
*Lagothrix
lagotricha*
(South
America)

MONKEY ON THE MARCH
The male mandrill lives mostly on
the forest floor. Females and young
climb up into low undergrowth.

TAIL GRIP
Tree-dwelling woolly monkeys
use their prehensile tails to grip
slippery branches in the canopy.

45

Hunters and killers

PREDATORS HAVE TO CATCH and kill other animals if they are to survive. They need to detect their prey before it sees them, to stalk, ambush or outrun it before it escapes, and incapacitate it before it can do them harm. To do all this, they must have acute senses. Daytime hunters often rely on their keen eyesight to find prey. Nocturnal hunters need other skills – a highly developed sense of hearing or smell, or an ability to detect vibrations made by an approaching animal. Prey animals have their own defences and means of avoiding capture, such as camouflage, so an incompetent hunter goes hungry.

AMBUSHED!
The solitary leopard *Panthera pardus* hunts by leaping on prey from above and killing it with a bite to the throat or neck.

Irritant hairs are kicked into face of assailant

Changeable hawk eagle
Spizaetus cirrhatus
(Southeast Asia)

HUNTER IN THE SKY
The changeable hawk eagle has exceedingly good eyesight so it can focus on an animal or bird on the distant ground. From its vantage-point, hidden in the foliage of a tall tree, this young bird of prey swoops down swiftly and silently, snatching up its victim with powerful talons.

DANGER ON EIGHT LEGS
As well as dry rocky places, the red-kneed tarantula lives in humid forests. During the day, it stays in its silk-lined burrow. After dark, it emerges to hunt for large insects or small vertebrates. It injects prey with a venom that quickly causes paralysis.

Red-kneed tarantula
Brachypelma smithi
(Central America)

Tough scaly skin protects the crocodile from flying hooves of prey

KILLER IN THE WATER
The Nile crocodile, together with the saltwater crocodile, is the largest of the jungle predators. It can reach a record 6 m (18 ft) in length, but even the smaller ones are powerful enough to overcome large animals – and people – that come down to the rivers in which it lives. Lurking unseen in the water, crocodiles are capable of surprising bursts of speed as they lunge forward to grab a drinking animal by the muzzle. They kill by dragging their catch under water until it drowns.

SMALL BUT DEADLY

The small common lancehead is nocturnal, locating warm-blooded prey with heat-sensitive pits between its eyes and nostrils. When a victim is in range, the snake gapes open its mouth, and two long front fangs swing forwards. As the snake strikes, these fangs stab, injecting a lethal venom. Most human deaths from snake bites in South America are due to this species.

Juvenile lures prey with yellow tail

Common lancehead
Bothrops atrox
(South America)

SQUEEZED TO DEATH

The boa constrictor waits motionless until its prey comes close enough, its air-borne scent picked up by the snake's tongue and transferred to the highly sensitive Jacobson's organs on the roof of its mouth. The snake strikes open-mouthed, gripping its catch with its fangs and coiling round the animal's body. Each time the animal breathes out, the snake tightens its coils a little more, until the prey is suffocated.

Boa constrictor
Boa constrictor
(Central and South America)

Formidable array of sharp teeth that are replaced continuously throughout the crocodile's life

Powerful jaws to swallow large prey

Nile crocodile
Crocodilus niloticus
(Africa)

TOOTH AND CLAW

The tiger *Panthera tigris* is a solitary animal that hunts by day or night. It stalks or ambushes, pouncing on its kill when it comes in range. Tigers can bring down deer or cattle with their formidably clawed fore-paws, and kill by biting. Although deer and goats are their usual diet, some tigers, particularly old or injured animals, take people.

Strong claws to climb quickly up slippery river banks

Tropical Asia

THE TERM "JUNGLE" is derived from a Hindi word "jangal", meaning impenetrable forest and undergrowth round settlements. Tropical Asia includes many countries and encompasses an enormous area. Part of this is continental mainland, but stretching south-east of this are the archipelagoes of Indonesia and Malaysia, some large, others tiny. It is a diverse and complex region, with many different peoples and histories. Much of the land is covered with tropical forest, including montane forests, and the evergreen and monsoon forests of the lowlands, all of which are rich in animal and plant life. With so much coastline, it is not surprising that most of the world's mangrove swamps are found here.

WORKING WITH PLANTS
Palm trees provide a plentiful raw material for many local industries. This Sarawak girl is splitting palm leaves into strips to be woven into matting or baskets.

Prominent eyes with vertical pupils for seeing in low light

TREE SNAKE
The nocturnal green cat snake (*Boiga cyanea*) lives almost exclusively in trees, often near water. It preys on other arboreal creatures, such as tree frogs and lizards. It subdues its prey with venom from fangs at the back of its mouth, before swallowing it whole.

INDIA

Bay of Bengal

China Sea

Malaysia

☐ *Former rainforest*
☐ *Actual rainforest*

Indonesia

Malayan tapir
Tapirus indicus

BROWSER
The tapir is a solitary animal that is most active at night. It browses with its long, mobile snout on leaves, fruits, and seeds in the thick jungle growth bordering water.

Strong legs for swimming

INDIA AND SOUTH-EAST ASIA
Many generations of human inhabitants have left little of the forest of mainland South-East Asia in its natural state. Some countries, such as Vietnam, are replanting. Some of the islands, notably in the Philippines, have lost all their rainforests. Others, such as Borneo, retain most of their original forest cover, parts of which are still unknown to outsiders.

48

Rattan palm
Calamus caesius

RATTAN PALMS
There are about 600
species of rattans. These
are climbing palms that
reach the canopy by means
of whips on the tips of the
fronds that are clothed
with hooked spikes. Rattan
canes are commercially
important for making
furniture that is exported
all round the world.

*Stem can reach
over 200 m
(660 ft) in length*

*Shape of petals
attracts insects*

*Leaf sheath covered
in hooked spines*

ONE OF THE FEW
There are about 70 species of
tropical slipper orchids, all of
which are found in South-East
Asia. Most of them grow on the
ground, but a few grow on trees
or rocks. Many slipper orchids are
naturally rare because they have
specific habitat requirements.
Since 1964, 20 new species have
been described, and *Paphiopedilum
primulinum* itself was only
discovered in 1972.

Flower bud

Slipper orchid
*Paphiopedilum
primulinum*

THE GINGER LILY
Many ginger lilies (*Hedychium spp.*) have fragrant,
attractive flowers, and their thick underground stems
often contain aromatic oils. After the tubular flower, a
fruit capsule develops, which when ripe splits to
reveal three rows of seeds.

Disguise and warning

ANIMALS AND INSECTS use camouflage in an effort to avoid being eaten. Colour and shape either make an animal indistinguishable from its background, or trick a predator into thinking that they are dealing with something bigger or more dangerous. Animals with cryptic coloration have colours or patterns that closely match their background. Some patterns seem bold and conspicuous, but actually break up an animal's outline, making it impossible to see against a mosaic of leaves, twigs, sunshine, and shadow. Mimicry takes this kind of camouflage a stage further, with insects looking like leaves, bark, or twigs. The disguise of many insects is so good that, rather than waste time looking for them, flocks of mixed species of birds move noisily through the forest like a wave. What small creatures one bird dislodges or disturbs, the bird behind snaps up.

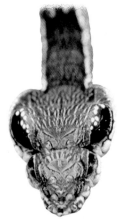

MIMICKING A SNAKE
When disturbed, the caterpillar of the hawkmoth *Leucorhampha ornatus* mimics a small, venomous pit-viper. It does this by swinging the front part of its body upside down, inflating its thorax to look like a snake's head.

False leaf katydid
Ommatopia pictifolia
(Central America)

STARTLE DISPLAY
The fore-wings of the false leaf katydid are near-perfect replicas of dead leaves. When motionless, it blends in well with low-growing vegetation. However, if it is discovered, this katydid has a second line of defence. In one quick movement, the fore-wings part to reveal a startling display of eye-spots. This should scare a predator long enough for the katydid to escape.

2 CHANGING COLOUR
The chameleon's colours intensify, with spots and stripes of purple quickly appearing. His tail straightens, and he takes up a more aggressive stance, puffing up his body to make it look bigger.

Parson's chameleon
Chamaeleo parsonii
(Africa)

1 REACTION TIME
Contrary to popular belief, a male chameleon does not change colour to match different backgrounds. But at the sight of a rival entering his territory, the response is immediate.

Each eye swivels independently, so the chameleon can look in two directions at the same time

COLOUR CHANGE IN CHAMELEONS
The skin of chameleons contains a small range of coloured pigments in specialized cells called chromatophores. Those that contain black pigment (melanin) lie deeper in the skin. When facing an intruder, there is a release of hormone from the pituitary gland. This triggers a surge of melanin pigment to the surface of the skin, and the skin colour darkens.

3 DARKER AND DARKER
His colour is now at its most intense. The red eyes and patches of red and green stand out against the deep blackish-purple. In an attempt to scare away the intruder, he hisses and lunges forward.

Warning coloration

Some poisonous animals and insects are conspicuously marked with bright colours and striking patterns that warn would-be predators, usually birds, that they taste awful. Often, the strategy is copied by non-poisonous species. It is known as Batesian mimicry, after Henry Walter Bates, the man who first described it. A change of colour is also used to communicate with a member of the same species. It can reflect a change of mood, scare off a rival, or signal to a potential mate during the breeding season.

Tiger moth
Ormeticia temporata
(Central America)

ALTERNATIVE DEFENCE
Moths and butterflies cannot sting attackers, or defend themselves by biting, unlike many other insects. Instead, they have to adopt other strategies. This tiger moth is well protected by its bold warning coloration. The bright yellow stripes on the wings act as a deterrent to any predators.

CAMOUFLAGED CAT
Light-coloured fur with dark stripes, spots, or blotches imitates the dappled effect of sunlight in the dense vegetation of the rainforest. It makes an effective camouflage for jungle cats. Tigers rely on their ability to remain unseen as they stalk an intended victim, until they are close enough to pounce.

Nectar-secreting gland

Leaf blade

Tricks and traps

Aт ALL LEVELS of the rainforest, there is a host of alert, wary creatures with a strong instinct for their own survival. A predator always has to outsmart its prey if it is to catch enough to eat. Some hunters combine trickery and deception with patience and the ability to move at lightning speed. Plants have a few mean tricks of their own. Sap-sucking insects may have their mouthparts gummed up by an unexpected flow of sticky latex. Other plants, that grow on poor or peaty soils, cannot get enough nutrients. In order to survive, some of these plants have turned carnivore.

Monkey cup
Nepenthes
mirabilis

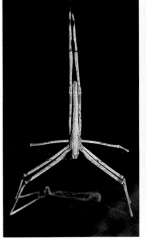

NETTED
Instead of waiting for an insect to fly into its web, the fishing-net spider (*Dinopus sp*) nets its prey. Suspended from lines of silk attached to a twig, it spins a small web of stretchy silk. Picking this up with its four front legs, it hangs upside down and waits. When an unsuspecting insect comes close, the spider drops the net over it.

SLIPPERY SLOPE
The rim of the pitcher plant is very slippery, so that small vertebrates and insects lose their footing and fall in. They are digested by enzymes in the liquid.

Pitcher develops at tip of leaf

Partly digested insects

Digestive gland

HUNGRY PLANT
Insects are attracted by the colour of the pitcher plants, and by nectar secreted around the rim. They are not aware, until it is too late, that it is a trap. They are digested by enzymes in the water half-filling each pitcher and are absorbed into the plant. The largest pitcher plants have pitchers 30 cm (12 in) long that hold 2 litres (4 pints) of liquid.

DEADLY LEAVES
The gaboon viper (*Bitis gabonica rhinoceros*) is patterned just like the sun-flecked leaves on the forest floor. It remains motionless and invisible until a small mammal or bird strays too close. Its 5 cm (2 in) long fangs inject a venom that is almost instantly fatal.

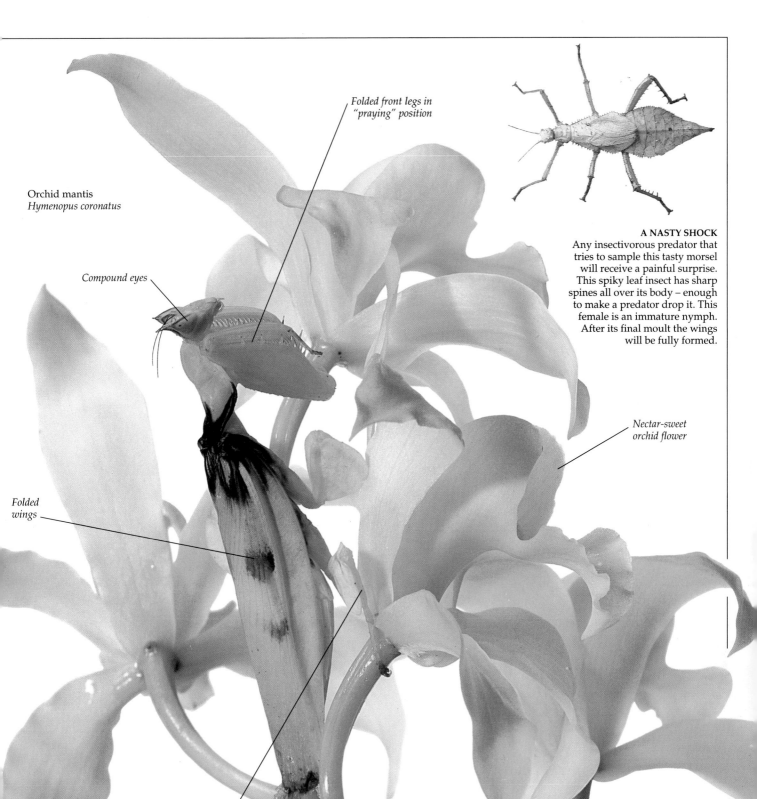

Folded front legs in
"praying" position

Orchid mantis
Hymenopus coronatus

Compound eyes

Folded
wings

Flap on back leg

A NASTY SHOCK
Any insectivorous predator that
tries to sample this tasty morsel
will receive a painful surprise.
This spiky leaf insect has sharp
spines all over its body – enough
to make a predator drop it. This
female is an immature nymph.
After its final moult the wings
will be fully formed.

*Nectar-sweet
orchid flower*

LADY IN WAITING
With her pale creamy colour and the petal-like flaps
on her legs, this female orchid mantis seems to be
part of the spray of blooms. She has two large
compound eyes at the corners of a triangular head
that swivel round while the rest of her body stays
still. When an insect visits the orchid, the mantis
takes deadly aim and strikes out with her front legs.

Flying high

LIVING IN THE CANOPY many metres above the ground is fine until an animal needs to travel from one tree top to the next in search of food or to escape a predator. Running down one tree trunk, along the ground, and up the next is hazardous and a waste of energy. Travelling through the air overcomes this, but only birds, bats, and insects have the wings and muscles that permit controlled flight. However, an assortment of other creatures have evolved ways of gliding through the air by increasing their body area, often with flaps of skin. When airborne, these flaps spread out like parachutes, increasing their wind resistance and slowing down the rate of descent. This prevents a damaging collision with the ground below. Many of these gliders can alter direction in mid-air by moving their legs, tail, or body, and some travel remarkable distances in this way.

FROG BEETLE
This Malayan frog beetle (*Sagra buqueti*) has its wings folded under wing cases called elytra.

BEETLING ABOUT
Before flying, this leaf beetle (*Doryphorella langsdorfii*) opens its elytra and spreads out its membranous wings.

FLYING GECKO
This nocturnal gecko (*Ptychozoon kuhli*) lives in trees and relies on camouflage to conceal it from predators. If it is spotted, it escapes by launching itself into the air and gliding to safety. Loose flaps of skin along each side and smaller flaps on its legs spread out and fill with air.

BIRDS OF PARADISE
The splendid plumage of male birds of paradise is used simply to attract a mate. Males gather in groups called leks in order to display. Some choose a high tree top and, as day breaks, give a colourful display, flashing their bright, iridescent plumage, and making loud calls.

Wide scales along tail

Flaps make lizard wider and flatter for gliding

Long legs for running

FLYING FROG
Reinwardt's flying frog (*Rhacophorus reinwardtii*) is one of a small number of rainforest tree frogs that leap out of a tree to escape from a pursuer. The digits of their very large hands and feet are connected by webs of skin. During long, gliding leaps, these behave like parachutes.

HUNTING WASP
The electric blue female hunting wasp (*Chlorion lobatum*) cruises low over the forest floor, hunting for crickets. It grips its prey with powerful jaws and paralyzes it with venom injected by its sting. It drags the insect into a burrow and lays a single egg in it, so that, on hatching, the larva has food until it pupates.

Webbing between toes

Blue-and-yellow macaw
Ara ararauna
(South America)

EXPERT PILOTS
Macaws have short, broad wings so
that they can fly skilfully between the
leafy branches of the forest canopy. They fly
considerable distances in search of trees bearing
ripe fruits. By changing the position of their wings
and tail feathers, they are also able to glide and brake
before landing on a branch or at a tree hole nesting site.

FLYING SNAKE
The flying tree snake (*Chrysopelea
pelias*) is one of five species from South-
East Asia that can glide through the air.
By raising its ribs upwards and outwards,
the snake flattens its body and so manages
to travel distances of up to 50 m (164 ft)
from one tree to another. When it lands on
the ground it resumes its usual shape.

Flying
dragon
Draco spp.

FLYING LIZARD
Flying dragons have six or
seven pairs of elongated
ribs covered with a
membrane of skin. These
"wings" are usually folded
against the lizard's body,
but open out so it can
glide long distances.

Wing
pattern and
colours help
males and
females find
each other

GIANT MOTH
The Atlas moth (*Attacus atlas*) is
one of the largest moths, with a
wingspan of 30 cm (12 in). Unlike
other insects, the wings of moths
and butterflies are covered with
minute, overlapping scales. These
are richly coloured, some because
they contain coloured pigments,
others because of the way that they
scatter the light that falls on them.

Australasian rainforests

ONE HUNDRED MILLION years ago, Australia was part of Antarctica, and rainforest covered the moist coastal regions of this vast southern continent. As Australia separated and drifted north, it became drier, and Antarctica colder. Australia's rainforests are all that is left of this ancient jungle, and contain some primitive flowering plants and conifers. Apart from the bats, all the native animals are pouch-bearing marsupials. New Guinea is to the north, a heavily forested island with a mixture of Asian and Australian plants and animals.

DANGER UNDERFOOT
The marbled scorpion (*Lychas marmoreus*) is found under bark and among leaf litter, where it hunts for small invertebrates. These are usually overpowered by the front claws and jaws. The venomous sting in the tail is used primarily for defence.

RARE AND BEAUTIFUL
Living only in a small area of the extreme south-east of Papua New Guinea, this is one of the world's most rare butterflies. It is also the largest, the female having a wingspan of up to 28 cm (11 in). These butterflies are found in the forest margins, but little is known about them.

The male is smaller than the female

Queen Alexandra's birdwing
Ornithoptera alexandrae

GREEN AND RED
The tiny flowers of this fig (*Ficus racemosus*) are contained in the fleshy green swellings that will eventually become sweet fruits. When the figs ripen, they turn red.

IN THE SHADE
This fleshy-stemmed fern lives beside water in shady forests. There is little strengthening tissue in the leaf stalks, and they soon wilt in dry conditions. *Angiopteris* ferns are very similar to the primitive ferns and tree ferns that were alive 325 to 280 million years ago, in the Upper Carboniferous period.

Long, arching leaf stalk

Angiopteris lygodiifolia

SOGERI SING-SING
In Papua New Guinea elaborate rituals and ceremonies such as the sing-sings have always been an important part of tribal life. New Guinea men adorn themselves with brightly coloured body paints, feathers, shells, and beads. Head dresses made with bird of paradise feathers are especially prestigious.

Doria's tree kangaroo
Dendrolagus dorianus

UP A TREE
Tree kangaroos have evolved from ground-living ancestors. They climb trees to browse on the foliage, but most kinds can still hop over the ground. Doria's tree kangaroo is the most arboreal. It has strong forelegs, broad hind feet, sharp claws and can no longer hop like other kangaroos. It lives in the cooler forests of the New Guinea highlands and has a thick fur coat to keep warm.

Sharp claws for climbing

New Guinea

AUSTRALIA

☐ *Former rainforest*
☐ *Actual rainforest*

AUSTRALASIA
New Guinea contains the largest expanse of rainforest to be found in South-East Asia. Most of it is still undisturbed, and many remote regions have yet to be explored. In contrast, Australian tropical rainforests are limited to patches in three main areas along the north-east coastal region .

FRIENDLY FROG
White's tree frog (*Litoria caerulea*) has round toe-pads that are sticky with mucus. It lives in forests, although it is familiar to many Australians because it also lives in water barrels and lavatories. It is 6-11 cm (2-4 in) long, and feeds on any moving creature small enough to swallow. These frogs spawn in still water, producing 200-2,000 eggs.

STICKY MEDICINE
The small tree *Ervatamia orientalis* grows in clearings and at the edges of Australian rainforests. When broken, the stems ooze a white, milky latex that some Aboriginals use to treat wounds and sores.

Jungle produce

FOR MANY CENTURIES, jungle products have been carried all round the world. A few, such as rubber, sugar, and chocolate, are now so much a part of everyday life, it is easy to forget their rainforest origins. Products with a world market are mostly grown in plantations. However, some, such as Brazil nuts, are still gathered from the forest. Many of the fruits and seeds that the tribespeople have enjoyed for a long time are only now beginning to find new markets in North America and Europe. In the future, we may be enjoying ice creams and using cosmetics that contain ever more exotic ingredients from the jungle.

NUTMEG PLANT
The red aril round the nutmeg seed is also used as a spice, called mace.

VAN HOUTEN'S
ROVA
COCOA
PURE SOLUBLE

A POPULAR FLAVOUR
Over 1,227,000 tonnes of cocoa beans are produced every year to manufacture chocolate, cocoa, drinking chocolate, and cocoa butter.

SPICING IT UP
Strongly flavoured spices such as pepper, ginger, cloves, and nutmeg were highly prized and very expensive in Europe in the Middle Ages. They were used to hide the tainted flavour of bad meat. Today, they are used to enhance the flavour of food, and to make medicines and toothpastes taste better. Spices are prepared from different parts of plants. For example, nutmeg is a seed, cloves are unopened flower buds, cinnamon comes from bark, and ginger is a root. They are dried and can be ground into a powder.

Ginger
Zingiber officinale

Cloves
Syzygium aromaticum

Nutmeg
Myristica fragrans

Cinnamon
Cinnamomum zeylanicum

COCOA BEANS
Cocoa trees have been cultivated for over 2,000 years in Central America. The Aztecs called the pods "cacahual", and believed that Quetzalcoatl, the plumed serpent god, dined on them. When ripe, cocoa pods are cut and split open by hand. The wet, pulpy mass of seeds is piled into baskets and allowed to ferment to lose unwanted pulp and develop the flavour. Then the seeds – the cocoa beans – are dried, cleaned, and polished, ready for export.

Cocoa pod
Theobroma cacao

Pulp

Rows of 20-60 oval seeds are embedded in a sweet pulp

Star fruit
Averrhoa carambola

Pineapple
Ananas comosus

STARFRUIT
Starfruits grow wild in Indonesian forests, but are planted widely in tropical Asia. They are an attractive garnish on food, as well as a source of vitamin C and iron.

SWEET POTATO
This starchy root *Ipomoea batatas* originated in tropical America and contains sugars, so it is pleasantly sweet. Sweet potatoes are boiled, roasted, or dried and ground into flour.

BREADFRUIT
The mass of flowers on this plant develop into the breadfruit which is 20-30 cm (8 in) across and can weigh as much as 2 kg (4 lb 4 oz). Its moist, starchy flesh is cooked as a vegetable.

RUBBER
Over 1,000 kinds of plants produce the white, sticky latex that can be made into rubber. The para rubber tree (*Hevea brasiliensis*) is by far the most important.

Pineapple cloth or piña

PINEAPPLE
Originating in South America, pineapples are now grown in many tropical countries. Both fresh and canned pineapples are popular foods, but the leaves have a different use. In the Philippines, thin fibres are extracted, prepared, spun and woven by hand to make a fine sheer cloth called piña. Piña shirts are part of the national costume.

Breadfruit
Artocarpus altilis

Large, sturdy prehensile tail

Explorers

THE LUCRATIVE spice market drew Portuguese, English, and Dutch explorers to the forested islands of South-East Asia in the 15th, 16th, and 17th centuries. At the same time, Spanish conquistadors were exploring Central America and Peru, interested more in ransacking Aztec and Inca gold than in the jungles. From the 16th century onwards, rival European nations fought to extend their empires in tropical regions. The 18th and 19th centuries saw a steady rise in scientific curiosity about these areas, with explorers such as Darwin and Wallace evolving the theories that have shaped modern thinking.

WILLIAM BLIGH (1754-1817)
For explorers who sailed the seas in bygone days conditions were harsh. In 1789, Captain Bligh was skipper of the *Bounty*, commissioned to transport young breadfruit trees from the tropical islands of Tahiti to the West Indies. His crew, who wanted to stay on Tahiti, rebelled and the famous mutiny took place. A second attempt succeeded and one of the trees planted by Bligh on St Vincent is still standing.

AIMÉ BONPLAND (1773-1858)
With von Humboldt, the Frenchman Aimé Bonpland explored both montane and lowland rainforests. Bonpland was a gifted artist and botanist, and recorded over 3,000 new species of plants, such as this *Melastoma coccinea*, in a splendid series of paintings.

Simia ursina painted by Baron von Humboldt

ALEXANDER VON HUMBOLDT (1769-1859)
This German naturalist landed in Venezuela in 1799, with Bonpland. Von Humboldt had a keen scientific interest in the animals, plants, and places he discovered.

IT'S ALL IN THE NAME
This woolly monkey, *Lagothrix lagotricha* (left) comes from the Orinoco and Upper Amazon basins. It is often called Humboldt's monkey to commemorate that intrepid explorer who had to put up with swarms of biting insects and fevers in this very humid region.

Livingstone's compass

Pages from one of Bates's notebooks

DAVID LIVINGSTONE (1813-1873)

Livingstone, a Scot, travelled to Africa to combine his missionary calling with exploration of the interior. He made three expeditions, travelling by river through dense forest, and mapping the Zambesi River and parts of the Nile.

CHARLES DARWIN (1809-1882)

Abandoning medicine and the priesthood, Darwin joined the crew of the *Beagle* in 1831. He was taken on to record the wildlife found during this small naval ship's mission to chart the South American coastline. The observations he made formed the basis for his theory of evolution.

Darwin's microscope

HENRY BATES (1825-1892)

In 1848, Henry Bates and his friend Alfred Wallace left safe jobs in England to explore the Amazon. In 11 years, Bates collected 14,000 specimens, mostly insects, of which 8,000 were new to science. He described how some harmless species mimic other poisonous ones; this is now known as Batesian mimicry.

Glass roof like greenhouse

BRINGING IT HOME

Transporting specimens back from the rainforests has always been difficult. This early 20th-century Wardian case (left) is a portable greenhouse used to carry plants safely back to the Royal Botanic Gardens at Kew, England. Plant specimens were also preserved by being pressed flat between sheets of absorbent paper. Succulent plants and fruits were preserved in spirits to stop them going mouldy.

YOUNG VENTURER

Since the 1970s, Colonel John Blashford-Snell has probably done most to enable biologists and young people to investigate the canopy. First in the Operation Drake, and then in the Operation Raleigh expeditions, they studied plants and animals from lightweight aluminium walkways many metres above the ground.

Under threat

Every year between one to two percent of the world's rainforest is cleared. The trees may be felled, often illegally, for logs and to clear land for farming. Some areas of rainforest have been polluted by mining activities. New roads have opened up once inaccessible regions, and people settling alongside them clear more land to grow crops. Conserving rainforests is one of the biggest challenges for environmentalists. At the current rate of deforestation, some scientists estimate that 17,000 species of rainforest plants and animals become extinct every year.

CLEARANCE FOR CATTLE RANCHING
In South and Central America, cleared tropical rainforest provides pasture for beef cattle. When ranchers move into the forest, they burn trees to clear the land for farming. After five years, each animal needs 5 hectares (12.5 acres) to graze. After 10 years the land is useless. Overgrazing, the impact of the animals' hooves, and the loss of the trees lead to soil erosion.

ENVIRONMENTAL INFLUENCES
Rainforests influence the carbon cycle and have a profound effect on rainfall. The uneven surface of tree tops causes air turbulence that increases the amount of water evaporating from the forest. This forms clouds that fall as rain. If the forests disappear, less rain will fall, it will drain more quickly, and air and soil temperatures will rise.

CO_2 removed from air during photosynthesis

CO_2 released into air during respiration of tree

Carnivore feeds on other animals

Leaves, branches and trunk built up from carbon-containing compounds

Droppings and remains from carnivorous animals

CO_2 released by respiring animals

Droppings and remains from herbivorous animals

Falling leaves and branches

CO_2 released from droppings and remains by decomposition

CO_2 released from leaf-litter by fungi and invertebrates

THE CARBON CYCLE
Green plants take up carbon dioxide, which they convert to sugars by means of photosynthesis, a process during which oxygen is released into the air.

Swallow-tailed manakin
Chiroxiphia caudata
(South and Central America)

VULNERABLE
Manakins live in the thickest forests and are not endangered at present. But their lifestyle and specialized diet of small soft fruits makes them vulnerable to forest disturbance.

THE OLD AND THE NEW
This beautiful Dutch mahogany armoire is an antique. Today, most of the mahogany that comes from Amazonia is poached, felled illegally at the expense of the lives and livelihood of the Amerindian tribespeople.

EMBROIDERED CLOTH, NILGIRI HILLS
In the Nilgiri Hills in India a large area of forest has been made into a Biosphere Reserve. Tribal groups are encouraged to live there in a traditional way, and supplement their livelihood by making items for export.

Maxillaria fulgens
(Central America)

HULI WIGMAN
Papua New Guinea has some of the least disturbed areas of rainforest. Many tribes live there, but the harmony with their surroundings is easily disrupted.

OBSESSIVE COLLECTION
Many of the estimated 18,000 species of orchids are found in rainforests. Their exotic blooms attract collectors, and the trade in these flowers, although frequently illegal, is worth a lot of money. Orchids are highly susceptible to over-collection and some face extinction in the wild.

Orang-utan
Pongo pygmaeus
(South-East Asia)

Arms are much longer than legs

Short fifth toe to help grip branches when swinging

NOWHERE TO LIVE
Selective logging removes target trees but leaves the rest. The increased light stimulates new growth, which benefits some animals, for instance leaf-eating primates that prefer young foliage. Others are not so adaptable. The adult orang-utan forages over a wide area on its own and is highly sensitive to disturbance. Like all other jungle creatures, this "man of the forest" has a right to survive.

Did you know?

AMAZING FACTS

Amazon

✳ Rainforests cover just 6 percent of the Earth's total land area, yet are home to over half the plant and animal species living on Earth.

✳ Half of the world's rainforests are within the borders of just three countries – Brazil in South America, Indonesia in South-East Asia, and Zaire in Africa.

✳ Tropical rainforests have an average temperature of around 25°C (77°F).

Motionless potoo guarding single egg in nest

Camouflaged potoo

✳ One hectare (2.5 acres) of jungle can support around 100 different kinds of tree. Some tropical forests have over 300.

✳ In the South American rainforest, one scientist discovered around 50 species of ants in one square metre of leaf litter.

✳ A rainforest's canopy is so dense that it blocks out around 98 percent of the Sun's light. Most animals live in this part of the forest.

✳ A sloth's fur has a green tinge because of the algae growing on it. Because it spends most of its time hanging upside-down, its fur is parted along its stomach rather than its back (as on other animals), helping rainwater to run off.

✳ The golden arrow poison frog found in the South American rainforest has enough venom in its skin to kill around 950 people.

✳ During the day, the common potoo of Central and South America camouflages itself by sitting in an upright posture, often on a broken branch or tree stump, with its head and bill pointing to the sky so it looks like part of the tree. It hunts for food at night.

✳ Some tree-top bromeliads can hold up to 55 litres (12 gallons) of water (about 8 sinkfuls!), providing a home to frogs, snakes, spiders, and even small mammals.

✳ Up to 80 different species of plant may live on a single emergent rainforest tree.

✳ Most of the world's 18,000–20,000 species of orchid live in tropical forests.

Golden arrow poison frog

✳ About 20 million hectares (50 million acres) of rainforest are lost every year – that's the size of England, Scotland, and Wales combined.

✳ One quarter of medicines used today are derived from plants. Drugs used to treat cancer, Hodgkin's disease, and other forms of leukaemia all come from rainforest plants.

Rainforest orchid
Odontoglossom laeve

Q Why are rainforest trees important to the Earth's climate?

A Rainforest trees – like all green plants – use carbon dioxide and produce oxygen when they make food from sunlight through photosynthesis. It is estimated that rainforests produce 50 percent of the Earth's oxygen. However, the main reason they affect our climate is that they hold vast stores of carbon in their leaves, stems, and roots. When they are burned or cut down and left to rot to clear land, the stored carbon is released into the atmosphere as carbon dioxide gas, contributing to the Greenhouse Effect.

Q Will the rainforest trees re-grow if they are cut down?

A If left undisturbed, rainforests will gradually re-grow. However, it is doubtful whether they will ever support the same variety of plants and animals. Re-growth happens naturally in forests when large trees die and fall to the ground, often taking smaller trees with them. As light pours into the "gap", fast-growing seeds and saplings grow upwards, with one tree eventually out-growing the rest. If huge areas of rainforest are cut down, however, the unprotected soil is eroded through heavy rains. Although new plants take root and grow, tall trees are unlikely to have enough soil and nutrients to grow into giants.

Cassowary of the Australasian rainforest

Collecting latex

Q Why do more types of animals live in rainforests than in any other habitat?

A Rainforests have existed for millions of years – some South-East Asian rainforests are around 100 million years old – so animals have had plenty of time to evolve. Conditions in the rainforests, with constant temperatures and plenty of rainfall, are ideal for sustaining a variety of animal life. Animals do not need to adapt to find ways to survive cold winters or to keep out of the hot sun, and they always have enough water.

Rainforest in Ecuador, cleared for oil exploration

Q What is sustainable farming and can it help save the rainforests?

A Sustainable use of the forest is the harvesting of rainforest products without affecting the rainforest's delicate balance of nature. For example, the Brazilian government has set aside land in which Brazil nuts can be harvested from the wild in a way that does not require deforestation. Similarly, latex can be collected from rubber trees without mass deforestation. These schemes not only help to save rainforest trees, they also provide an income for indigenous peoples. However, much more needs to be done. Wood is a renewable resource and many environmental groups now back schemes for the sustainable use of the world's forests.

Record Breakers

✳ **LARGEST JUNGLE BIRD**
The cassowary of the Australasian rainforest grows up to 1.5 m (5 ft) tall.

✳ **LARGEST JUNGLE FLOWER**
The giant rafflesia of South-East Asia can grow around 1 m (3 ft) wide and weigh up to 7 kg (15.4 lb).

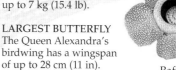

✳ **LARGEST BUTTERFLY**
The Queen Alexandra's birdwing has a wingspan of up to 28 cm (11 in).

Rafflesia

✳ **LONGEST JUNGLE SNAKE**
The anaconda of South America grows to an average length of 5.5 m (18 ft).

Endangered jungle animals

Here are just a few rainforest animals that are endangered because of poaching and loss of habitat. Some are now critically endangered, meaning they face an extremely high risk of extinction in the wild*.

Philippine eagle

Common gibbon

AYE AYE
Daubentonia madagascariensis
Habitat and range: Protected rainforest on the African island of Madagascar
Status: Endangered
Numbers: Estimated population of less than 2,500; numbers are expected to halve over the next 10 years based on current rate of habitat loss.
Reasons for decline: Habitat loss through logging and conversion to agriculture; the aye aye has also often been killed by local people who consider a sighting of the animal to be a harbinger of misfortune.

PHILIPPINE EAGLE
Pitheccophages jefferyi
Habitat and range: Rainforests in Indonesia and the Philippines (the eagle is the national bird of the Philippines)
Status: Critically endangered
Numbers: There are thought to be possibly fewer than 250 mature birds in the wild; attempts are now being made to breed the eagle in captivity and return it to its natural habitat.
Reasons for decline: Erosion of habitat through logging and clearing land for agriculture.

Aye aye

Long arms for swinging and reaching fruit

JAVAN SILVERY GIBBON
Hylobates moloch
Habitat and range: Rainforest of western and central Java in South-East Asia
Status: Critically endangered
Numbers: There are thought to be just 2,000 Javan gibbons in fragmented populations in the wild. Other species of gibbon, such as the common (or lars) gibbon, are currently considered low risk because there are around 300,000 remaining in their native habitat. However, if current rates of deforestation continue, they may also become vulnerable and even endangered with extinction.
Reasons for decline: Loss of habitat through deforestation for farming, logging, and mining.

Sumatran tiger

SUMATRAN ORANG-UTAN
Pongo abelii
Habitat and range: Rainforests of Sumatra in South-East Asia
Status: Critically endangered
Numbers: There are thought to be just 15,000 to 20,000 orang-utans (*Pongo pygmaeus* and *Pongo abelii*) remaining in the wild.
Reasons for decline: Poaching and loss of habitat; some animals are also captured for the illegal pet trade.

SUMATRAN TIGER
Panthera tigris ssp *sumatrae*
Habitat and range: Sumatran forest, including tropical forest
Status: Endangered
Numbers: There are thought to be only around 400 animals remaining in the wild, in Sumatra's five national parks.
Reasons for decline: Loss of habitat, poaching, and the illegal trade in tiger parts for use in traditional Chinese medicine. The other three subspecies of tiger are also endangered.

Adult orang-utans are solitary animals, ranging over several kilometres of rainforest

* Based on data from the 2002 Red List of Threatened Species™. For up-to-date information, log on to www.redlist.org/

Sumatran orang-utan

Hyacinth macaw

Bonobo

GORILLA
Gorilla gorilla
Habitat: Central Africa, in small areas of wild forest and reserves
Status: All gorillas (eastern, western, and mountain) are now endangered.
Numbers: There are thought to be around 40,000 western lowland gorillas remaining in the wild. The eastern lowland gorilla, now found only in the Democratic Republic of Congo, is thought to have a population of 3,000–5,000. The mountain gorilla is the most endangered, with only 670 animals remaining in the wild. Half of this number live in protected areas of the Virunga volcanic region of Rwanda, Uganda, and the Democratic Republic of Congo. The rest live in Bwindi National Park in Uganda.
Reasons for decline: Loss of forest home due to logging or clearing land for ranches, farms, and plantations. Civil unrest in some African countries has also made it difficult to patrol reserves and safeguard animals from poachers, who hunt gorillas for their meat and skins. Hunting gorillas and other wild animals in the forests of the Congo Basin in Africa is so excessive that poaching is considered to be more of a threat to animal conservation than deforestation.

HYACINTH MACAW
Anodorhynchus hyacinthinus
Habitat and range: South American rainforest in Brazil, Bolivia, and Paraguay
Status: Endangered
Numbers: Around 2,500–5,000 birds in three distinct populations.
Reasons for decline: Trade (considered a prized pet), hunting, and deforestation.

Mountain gorilla from Rwanda

BONOBO (PYGMY CHIMPANZEE)
Pan paniscus
Habitat and range: Remote rainforests of central Zaire in Africa
Status: Endangered (along with other kinds of chimpanzee, such as the western chimpanzee)
Numbers: Estimates suggest there are 10,000–15,000 left in the wild.
Reasons for decline: Hunting for its meat and the sale of young as pets.

Hunted to extinction

Rhino horns

Many countries have passed laws banning the hunting of endangered animals, and have set aside national parks and reserves to preserve what remains of their habitats. However, even though it is illegal, many endangered animals, such as the orang-utan, tiger, and rhinoceros, are still poached for their meat and hides. Sometimes mothers are killed so that their young can be captured and sold as pets.

Young primates are also caught and sold for medical research. Many endangered animals are also hunted because their body parts are though to have healing powers in traditional Chinese medicine. For example, a tiger's whiskers are sold to ease toothache, its tail is used to treat skin diseases, and its bones are thought to help cure rheumatism.

SUMATRAN RHINOCEROS
Dicerorhinus sumatrensis
Habitat and range: Lowland rainforests of South-East Asia
Status: Critically endangered
Numbers: It is estimated that there are less than 300 animals remaining in the wild, in the forests of Indonesia and Malaysia. The Javan rhinoceros is also critically endangered, with just 60 animals left in the lowland rainforests of Ujung Kulon National Park on Java, Indonesia, and Cat Tien National Park in Vietnam.
Reasons for decline: Deforestation, and poaching for its highly priced horn, which is thought to have medicinal properties.

Sumatran rhinoceros

Find out more

THERE IS A WEATH OF INFORMATION AVAILABLE about the world's jungles. Maybe one day you will be fortunate enough to explore a rainforest. Until then, see jungle animals up close in local zoos and wildlife centres, and find out about their captive breeding programmes and other important conservation work. You can also watch wildlife programmes on television, get online to access information over the internet, join a conservation group, or visit a botanical garden.

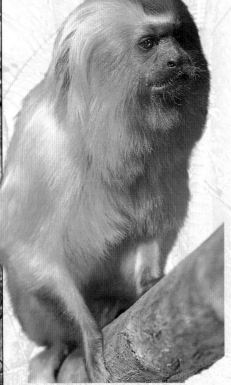

Golden lion tamarin

ZOOS AND WILDLIFE CENTRES

Find out about your nearest zoo's conservation work. It may be involved in breeding and raising endangered animals. In the 1970s, the golden lion tamarin was thought to be the world's most endangered primate, with only around 100 animals left in the wild. Since then, captive breeding programmes in zoos worldwide and the setting up of forest reserves have increased populations, and the golden lion tamarin now has a much greater chance of survival.

ECOTOURISM

It is now easier to visit some of the world's rainforests through ecotourism. Ecotourism means to visit a place to sightsee or learn about its natural environment without, for example, staying in a plush hotel and using up valuable water resources. While ecotourism in the world's rainforests does not directly help to save the forests, money spent by tourists can be used for conservation work, reforestation, management of reserves, and so on. However, care must be taken not to upset the ecosystem's delicate balance of nature, so tourism must be carefully managed, and visitor numbers limited.

Ecotourism in Malaysian rainforest

The Dian Fossey
Gorilla Fund
International

Ecotourists in
Rwanda, Africa

ADOPT AN ANIMAL

Many zoos and conservation organizations enable you to adopt an animal by making a contribution towards its upkeep. For example, through the Dian Fossey Gorilla Fund International (an organization that continues the work of Dian Fossey, a scientist who dedicated her life to saving mountain gorillas), you can adopt a gorilla from the Karisoke Research Centre in Rwanda. When you adopt an animal, you receive a photo and adoption papers and can keep track of the animal over the website (http://www.gorillafund.org/).

Places to visit

EDEN PROJECT, ST AUSTELL, CORNWALL
Eden houses a huge collection of plants from all over the world. Highlights in the Humid Tropics biome include:
• a complete Malaysian stilt house made from plants (including bamboo and rattan that surround it)
• a rare ebony plant from Oceania

ROYAL BOTANIC GARDENS, KEW, SURREY, ENGLAND
Kew has hundreds of botanical specimens including many species of tropical trees, shrubs, and plants. Look out for:
• rattan palms, epiphytic plants, breadfruit and banana trees in the Palm House
• cycads, which are on the verge of extinction in many habitats

NATURAL HISTORY MUSEUM, LONDON
See thousands of exhibits of animals from all over the world. Highlights include:
• the Darwin Centre, which houses 22 million preserved animal specimens collected during the last 300 years, including some of those brought back to England by explorers in the 18th and 19th centuries, including Darwin himself
• the Life Galleries, with permanent exhibits on mammals and primates, and ecology

Rattan palm

LONDON ZOO, REGENT'S PARK, LONDON
Find out about the zoo's work in animal conversation and see:
• Sumatran tigers, which are part of a European captive breeding programme
• the Macaw Aviary, including endangered Hyacinth macaws

WHIPSNADE WILD ANIMAL PARK, BEDFORDSHIRE
This wildlife park has over 2,500 animals living in open paddocks or roaming free in parkland. Look out for the three species of rhinoceros (Black, White, and Asian) threatened with extinction, now bred in the park.

CONSERVATION MATTERS
Contact an environmental group to see what it is doing to try to save and protect the world's rainforests and find out how you can help. Many of these groups have websites (see box below) and produce information such as factsheets, films, and brochures. They also raise money and campaign for stricter environmental laws. Help to save rainforest trees by using less paper. As well as recycling paper, write on both sides of every sheet you use, and try to use cloth napkins and towels instead of paper napkins and towels.
Check out the Rainforest Action website (www.ran.org) for plenty of information on recycling as well as wood-free paper options using waste straw, kenaf, or hemp.

Recycling newspapers and magazines

USEFUL WEBSITES

▸ Conservation groups:
http://www.rainforest.org/
http://www.rainforest-alliance.org/

▸ Homepage of the Worldwide Fund for Nature, with information on where to join and other WWF websites:
http://wwf.org/

• London Zoo, with links to animal adoption:
http://londonzoo.com

• For information on rhinos:
http://www.sosrhino.org/

Queen Alexandra birdwing butterfly

BUTTERFLY GARDENS
Large butterfly gardens often have a tropical hothouse where you can see colourful rainforest species flitting through the trees. The London Butterfly House at Syon Park, Brentford, has 500–1200 butterflies, with species from Costa Rica, Indonesia, Thailand, and the Philippines.

Hexagons in domed roof made up of layers of inflated transparent foil, each 2 m (6 ft) deep

EDEN PROJECT
The Humid Tropics Biome at the Eden Project in Cornwall, England, is the largest conservatory in the world, containing over 1,000 plant species from the jungles of Malaysia, West Africa, the islands of Oceania, and South America. Misters and waterfalls inside the dome keep the air moist, and the air is regulated so it is between 18°–35°C (64.4°–95°F), recreating the heat and humidity of a tropical forest. As well as experiencing what it is like to walk through jungle plants, you can also learn about the hundreds of uses of plants in our everyday lives. More information about the Eden Project and news about current exhibitons and workshops can be found on its website (www.edenproject.com).

Inside the Humid Tropics Biome at the Eden Project

Glossary

ADAPTATION Process by which a living organism gradually changes genetically so that is becomes better suited to a particular environment.

AMPHIBIAN Ectothermic (cold-blooded) vertebrate such as a frog, whose young uses gills to breathe during its early stages of life.

BIODIVERSITY (or biological diversity) The wide variety of living organisms, including plant and animal life.

BIOME Large ecological unit broadly corresponding to one of the world's major climatic regions, such as a tropical forest, desert, and so on.

BIOSPHERE All the habitats on Earth.

BROMELIAD Member of a family of plants, many of which are epiphytes that live on the boughs of trees. (*see also* EPIPHYTE)

BUTTRESS ROOT Supporting structure that grows from the base of a tree's trunk, helping to support its weight.

CAMOUFLAGE An animal's colour or pattern that enables it to blend in with its surroundings in order to hide from predators or lie in wait for prey.

CANOPY Layer in a forest that is made up of the leafy crowns of most trees.

CARBON DIOXIDE Colourless, odourless gas given out by animals and plants during respiration, which is absorbed by plants during photosynthesis. Too much carbon dioxide gas in the atmosphere results in global warming. (*see also* GLOBAL WARMING)

Bromeliad

CARNAUBA Type of high-quality wax taken from wax palms, used mainly in the cosmetics and polishes industries.

CINCHONA Plant from which quinine is obtained, which is sometimes used in the treatment of malaria.

CLIMATE The pattern of weather in a particular place over a long period of time.

CLOUD FOREST Type of rainforest growing at high altitudes enveloped by permanent heavy mist, and usually covered by a thick layer of moss and liverwort.

CONSERVATION Protecting, preserving, and managing the Earth's natural resources and its environment.

CURARE Type of poison used by some South American tribespeople to coat their arrow tips when hunting prey.

CYCAD Palm-like, seed-bearing plant with long fern-like leaves.

Emergent tree breaking through the canopy

DEFORESTATION When forest is felled and cleared as a result of human activity.

ECOLOGY The scientific study of plants and animals in relation to their environment, or ecosystem.

ECOSYSTEM A community of living organisms in their natural habitat, forming an interdependent food chain. (*see also* BIOME)

EMERGENT Very tall tree that towers above the rest of the rainforest canopy. (*see also* CANOPY)

ENDANGERED In danger of extinction.

EPIPHYTE Plant that grows on another plant (often a tree) for support, and often to reach the light. Epiphytes absorb nutrients from rain and debris lodged on the bark of the tree.

EXTINCTION The dying out of a plant or animal species.

Kapok fibre

Kapok pod

FOOD CHAIN Series of plants and animals linked by their feeding relationships.

FOOD WEB A series of several interlinked food chains.

GERMINATION Process in which a seed starts to grow.

GLOBAL WARMING Warming of the Earth's atmosphere caused by a build-up of greenhouse gases. (see also CARBON DIOXIDE, GREENHOUSE EFFECT)

GREENHOUSE EFFECT The accumulation of gases such as carbon dioxide in the atmosphere, which allows sunlight to reach the Earth's surface but prevents heat leaving.

Primate

HABITAT Environment or surroundings in which an organism (plant or animal) lives.

HUMIDITY The amount of water vapour in the air. A tropical rainforest has an average humidity of around 82 percent.

HUMUS Decomposed organic matter.

KAPOK Light, waterproof, oily fibre covering the seeds of some species of silk-cotton tree; often used for stuffing pillows.

LATEX Thick, milky juice produced by some plants, including the rubber tree, the sap of which is used in the manufacture of rubber products.

LIANA Plant with a long, slender stem that climbs or twines up jungle trees or dangles down from the canopy so its leaves can reach the light.

LICHEN Plant-like organism formed from a partnership between a fungus and an alga or cyanobacterium, which forms crusts and tufts on trees, rocks, or soil.

LITTER Dead leaves, twigs, and branches that fall to, and carpet, the forest floor.

LIVERWORT Plant related to moss; some have a lobed plant-body that resembles a liver; once used to treat liver diseases.

MAMMAL Endothermic (warm-blooded), hairy vertebrate that suckles its young.

MANGROVE Tree that grows in muddy swamps covered at high tide, or on tropiccal coasts and the shores of estuaries; characterized by long, tangled roots.

MARSUPIAL Animal in which the young is usually carried in a pouch by the female.

MIMICRY Copying the behaviour, colouring, or markings of another more dangerous animal to escape from predators.

MONSOON Wind that changes direction according to the seasons; also used to mean the heavy seasonal rains it brings to parts of the world.

MOSS Small plant with simply constructed leaves, attaching itself to the earth, trees or rock by short, rootlike hairs.

NOCTURNAL Active by night rather than by day (diurnal).

NUTRIENT Food needed by plants and animals to live and grow.

POACHER Hunter who kills an animal illegally. Some commercial poachers use shotguns, rifles or even machine guns to kill their prey. Others use more traditional weapons, such as spears or arrows.

PHOTOSYNTHESIS The process by which green plants produce food by using the energy from sunlight to build simple sugars from carbon dioxide and water.

PREHENSILE Flexible part of the body (usually the tail) that is able to grip. For example, some monkeys have prehensile tails, which are used like another hand, to hold branches.

PRESERVATION Keeping something from harm or decay.

Liana

PRIMATE An order in the animal kingdom, including monkeys, apes and human beings.

REPTILE Ectothermic (cold-blooded) scaly vertebrate (animal with a backbone) that reproduces by laying eggs or giving birth on land. Living reptiles include lizards, snakes, turtles and crocodiles.

SLASH AND BURN AGRICULTURE When land is cleared by slashing trees and bushes then burning them to release nutrients into the soil. The cleared land is usually used for farming or for raising cattle.

SPECIES A distinct group of plants or animals that can breed successfully with a member of the same group to produce fertile offspring.

STILT ROOT Long root growing from the lower part of a trunk, giving a plant support on difficult terrain, such as steep slopes.

STRANGLER FIG Type of plant that starts life as an epiphyte, growing on a tree-top branch. Its long aerial roots eventually grow down to the ground, covering the tree until the tree dies and rots away.

Tendril

TENDRIL Coil-like shoot from a climbing plant that enables it to cling to another plant and climb towards the light.

TRANSPIRATION Release of water into the air from green plants during the process of photosynthesis (making food from sunlight).

TROPICAL To do with the tropics – the hot, wet regions lying on or near the equator, between the Tropic of Cancer that lies on the line of latitude 23.5° north of the equator, and the Tropic of Capricorn that lies on the line of latitude 23.5° south of the equator.

Tuber of a sweet potato

TUBER Swollen root or underground stem-tip that contains a reserve of food (usually sugars and starches).

UNDERSTOREY Layer of vegetation below the rainforest canopy where limited sunlight penetrates.

VENOM Toxic liquid used by an animal to paralyze or kill its prey.

Index

Acknowledgments

The publisher would like to thank:
Mark Alcock; the staff of the Royal Botanic Gardens, Kew, in particular Jenny Evans, Doris Francis, Sandra Bell, Phil Brewster, Dave Cooke, John Lonsdale, Mike Marsh, and John Norris; David Field and Sue Brodie of ECOS, the Royal Botanic Gardens, Kew; Mark O'Shea, herpetologist, and Nik Brown and Pete Montague of the West Midland Safari Park; the staff and keepers of Twycross Zoo, in particular Molly Badham, Donna Chester, and John Ray; Robert Opie, Jim Hamill, Jane Beamish, and Mike Row, British Museum, Museum of Mankind; Martin Brendell of the Natural History Museum; Janet Boston of the Liverpool Museum; Helena Spiteri for editorial help; Susan St Louis, Isaac Zamora, Ivan Finnegan, and Sarah Cowley for design help.
Maps by John Woodcock
Additional photography by Peter Anderson (38-39); Geoff Brightling (33tr); Jane Burton/Kim Taylor (17cl and cr, 33cl); Peter Chadwick (16cr); Frank Greenaway (12tl, 23tr and br, 28tl and bl, 29tl, 35cl, 37tr, 52b, 53b, 54c, 55b, 56cr); Colin Keates (7cr, 54tl); Dave King (58b); Cyril Laubscher (7tr); Karl Shone (32-33, 62bl); Kim Taylor (40tr, 50-51); Jerry Young (16cl, 17b, 23br, 29bl, 31tr, 35tl, 53tr, 63b)

Index by Hilary Bird

The publisher would like to thank the following for their kind permission to reproduce their photographs:

Picture credits
a-above; b-below; c-centre; l-left; r-right; t-top
Bridgeman Art Library/Royal Botanic Gardens, Kew: 18bl, 35c; /Leiden, Rijksmuseum voor Volkenkunde: 38 bc; /British Museum: 39tr; /Royal Geographical Society: 60br; /Bonhams: 62bc
Bruce Coleman Ltd: 9tl; /M.P.L.Fogden: 12tr; /G.B.Frith: 15tl; /Konrad Wothe: 16c; /Jane Burton: 27tl; /D.Houston: 28br; /WWF/H.Jungius: 33tl; /Dieter and Mary Plage: 36bl; /Peter Ward: 37bl; /Dieter and Mary Plage: 46tr
Corbis: Michael S. Lewis 68b; Tom Stewart 69tr.
Mary Evans Picture Library: 46tl
Michael & Patricia Fogden: 6bc, 13br, 13bl, 14c, 14tr, 35tr, 51bl, 63tr
Dian Fossey Gorilla Fund International: 68c.
Robert Harding Picture Library: 30lc, 34tr, 39tl, 62tl, 63tc
Hutchison Library /Isabella Tree: 39br; /Dr Nigel Smith: 42br

Frank Lane Picture Agency/E.& D. Hosking: 11tl; /Silvestris: 31bl
Mansell Collection: 60tr
Natural History Museum, London: 59, 69cra.
N.H.P.A.: /Morten Strange: 8tl; /Otto Rogge: 15r; /Stephen Dalton: 24cr, 33cr; /Kevin Schafer: 43tl; /G.I.Bernard: 50cr; /Stephen Kraseman: 50tr; /Alberto Mardi 69br; /Daryl Balfour 67cl; /Gerard Lacz 67br; /Jany Sauvanet 65tc; /Kevin Schafer 70tc; /Mark Bowler 65cr, 66bl; /Martin Wendler 64tl; /Michael Leach 64bl.
N.H.P.A.Planet Earth Pictures: /Andre Bartschi 8bl; /Peter Scoones: 9tr; /Andrew Mounter: 21tl; /John Lythgoe: 22bl; /Anup Shah: 47br; /David Maitland: 56tr; /Mary Clay: 57bc
Nature Picture Library: /Anup Shah 66br, 67cr; /Bruce Davidson 64-65; /John Cancalosi 71cr; /Morley Read 65b; /Neil Lucas 66tr; /Pete Oxford 66tl; /Staffan Widstrand 71bc; /Stefan Widstrand 70-71; /Sue Daly 64tr.
Oxford Scientific Films: /Harold Taylor 66-67, 70bl; /Konrad Wothe 67tr; /Martyn Colbeck 67tl; /Paul Franklin 68-69; /Philip Tull 68tl; /Steve Turner 71tl.
Panos Pictures /Fred Hoogervorst 68cr.

Premaphotos Wildlife/K.G.Preston-Mafham: 49br, 56lc, 57br
Raleigh International Picture Library /Chris Rainier: 61br
Harry Smith/Polunin Collection: 10tr
Still Pictures/Edward Parker: 6tl; /Norbert Wu: 29tr, 52tr
Survival Anglia /Frances Furlong: 40bc; /M.Kavanagh: 48tr
Syndication International: 58tl; /Natural History Museum: 60cr c.Alan Watson/Forest Light: 8cr
M.I.Walker/Microworld Services: 18bc

Every effort has been made to trace the copyright holders and we apologise in advance for any unintentional omissions. We would be pleased to insert the appropriate acknowledgment in any subsequent edition of this publication.

All other images © Dorling Kindersley.
For further information see:
www.dkimages.com